HBR Guide to
Managing Up
and Across

Harvard Business Review Guides

Arm yourself with the advice you need to succeed on the job, from the most trusted brand in business. Packed with how-to essentials from leading experts, the HBR Guides provide smart answers to your most pressing work challenges.

The titles include:

HBR Guide to Better Business Writing

HBR Guide to Finance Basics for Managers

HBR Guide to Getting the Mentoring You Need

HBR Guide to Getting the Right Job

HBR Guide to Getting the Right Work Done

HBR Guide to Giving Effective Feedback

HBR Guide to Making Every Meeting Matter

HBR Guide to Managing Stress

HBR Guide to Managing Up and Across

HBR Guide to Persuasive Presentations

HBR Guide to Project Management

HBR Guide to
Managing Up and Across

HARVARD BUSINESS REVIEW PRESS

Boston, Massachusetts

Library of Congress Cataloging-in-Publication Data

Guide to managing up and across.

    p. cm. — (Harvard business review guides)

  Includes index.

  ISBN 978-1-4221-8760-9 (alk. paper)

  1. Managing your boss.   2. Management—Psychological aspects.

3. Interpersonal relations.

  HF5548.83.G85 2012

  650.1'3—dc23

                                   2012025301

The paper used in this publication meets the requirements of the American National Standard for Permanence of Paper for Publications and Documents in Libraries and Archives z39.48-1992.

What You'll Learn

Does your boss make you want to scream? Do you have more than *one* boss? Do you spend your day herding cats? Working across departmental silos? Corralling contractors?

Then you know that managing up and across your company is critical to doing your job well. It's all about understanding your boss's and colleagues' priorities, pressures, and work styles. You need to manage up and across not just because you may have a problem boss, incompetent colleagues, or projects that involve stakeholders flung far and wide. You need to manage up and across, for example, to get your marketing and sales folks to see that *your* project will help them meet *their* goals, too; to establish authority with higher-ups so they'll bless your new product ideas; to secure people's time for a new team when they're already feeling overextended.

Managing up and across will help you get the information and resources you need to solve your complex problems, increase your effectiveness, and make your work more enjoyable.

You'll get better at:

- Getting what you need from people who don't report to you

- Coping with micromanaging, conflict-aversive, or generally incompetent bosses

- Discovering what drives colleagues of all ages

- Partnering with your boss—and *her* boss

- Selling your ideas up and across your company

- Making the most of your boss's influence

- Establishing a shared vision and commitment

- Juggling multiple bosses' priorities

- Tailoring your pitch to your audience

- Collaborating with remote colleagues

- Working with a new boss

- Navigating office politics

Contents

Section 1: MANAGING UP

Contents

Section 2: MANAGING ACROSS

Contents

Section 1
Managing Up

Neglecting to manage up may cost you promotions or chances to put your great ideas into action. But understanding what makes your boss and his cohort tick and embracing their priorities will open doors for you.

This isn't kissing up or manipulation. You're not trying to inflate egos. You're helping the people you work for succeed, which in turn helps you succeed.

This section of the guide is about creating win-win relationships with higher-ups. You'll learn how to present problems and opportunities to them, give them feedback, connect with your boss's boss without doing an end run, and deal with a variety of difficult managers—from the micromanager to the conflict-averse.

Managing Your Boss

by Linda A. Hill and Kent Lineback

Managing *up* is important because your boss plays a pivotal role in your success—or your failure. You can leverage your boss's influence in the organization on your behalf in several ways—for example, by obtaining valuable information, winning needed resources, and securing important support for your personal development and career. When you face difficult trade-offs and must make decisions that create both beneficial and painful consequences for others, your boss's advice, insight, knowledge of the organization, and access to higher management can be invaluable. As your organization shifts and changes shape in an uncertain market, a good relationship here

Adapted from *Being the Boss: The 3 Imperatives for Becoming a Great Leader* (product #12285), by Linda A. Hill and Kent Lineback, Harvard Business Review Press, 2011 becomes a necessity for navigating through the turmoil. The penalties of a poor relationship are many: less influence, little information or advice, fewer resources, and limited personal development and career support. Worst case, you can find yourself isolated, ignored, pushed out—your journey stalled, your career derailed.

Why Is It Often an Uneasy Relationship?

This relationship can be problematic for two reasons. First, a boss plays conflicting roles: supporter and evaluator, which can create confusion. Second, people often bring their past experience with authority into the relationship, which can create unnecessary complications.

This is an area where being a star as an individual contributor may not have prepared you for management. As an exceptional performer, you probably had minimal interaction with your boss. If so, you most likely didn't develop the skills of managing up that you need.

Do you see your boss as coach and developer or as evaluator and judge?

You're caught in a difficult dilemma, one that can feel personally threatening. The boss is not only a potential source of great help, in both your job and your career, but also the one who evaluates your performance. To get help from her as a developer, particularly with your personal development, you must reveal your shortcomings. But if you do, she in her role as evaluator may interpret your weaknesses as serious faults. Many managers handle this dilemma by striving to appear capable and in control even when they're not. They see their boss more as threat than ally and lose the potential benefits of her help.

Are you confused by your boss's dual role? Do you tend to see your boss as primarily a judge? Does that attitude seem safer to you? That's understandable, but it's not always the most helpful point of view.

What can you do? Don't presume your boss is always one or the other, judge or coach. Instead, think of his dual roles as extremes between which he moves back and forth depending on the situation. At first, in small ways that aren't risky, test his willingness to provide support. That way, you can see when, where, and how he's likely to focus on development rather than evaluation. Learn his feelings about what's important in management—such as careful planning, decisiveness, building consensus— and make sure you develop and display those qualities.

Do you see past bosses in your current boss?

How do you feel about your current boss? How do you respond to authority in general and to those who have it? If most of your bosses have frustrated you and fallen short of your expectations, you and they may be victims of the emotional baggage you carry forward from past experience. Reflect on your own history and the feelings it's created in you. That history may lead you to perceive your current boss not as who she is but as an amalgam of past authority figures, with all the positive and negative feelings that flow from that past. Unless you're aware of these feelings, you'll be at their mercy.

On the other hand, you may respond to authority with overdependence, rather than resistance. Extreme

WHAT YOUR BOSS EXPECTS OF YOU

You and your boss agree on your annual, individual performance targets that support larger organizational goals. But what about her *undocumented* expectations? What should you be doing beyond your formal job description that will make you indispensable to your boss and your organization as a whole?

- *Collaborate.* Overcome differences between you and others so you work together effectively—even if you don't like each other.

- *Lead initiatives.* Don't be reluctant to associate yourself with unproven ideas, especially those that cross functional or unit boundaries. Raise your hand, and you'll climb the ladder faster than those who don't.

- *Develop your own people.* Take as active an interest in your employees' development as you do in your own—if not more. Go out of your way to criticize and praise your people when they need it. And during performance reviews, supply people with specific, candid, and useful feedback.

- **_Stay current._** Regularly read and watch the news. What happens in the world affects what happens with your team, your marketplace, and your competition. Also know what's going on with your customers—how they're changing, how their competition is changing, and how technology and world events are affecting their strategies. Your customer relationships are key assets: Bring them to the table.

- **_Drive your own growth._** Seek perpetual education and development—not necessarily by going to school but by finding exposure to new people and ideas. Seek feedback from your boss, and accept demanding assignments.

- **_Be a player for all seasons._** Demonstrate positive behaviors even during hard times. You'll sustain your ability to motivate and inspire your own people no matter what's going on around you.

Adapted from "What Your Leader Expects of You" (product #R0704C) by Larry Bossidy, _Harvard Business Review,_ April, 2007 deference and automatic, unquestioning compliance don't work well either. Those who react this way never disagree or push back, even when they're right or it's in their best interest.

Both antagonism to authority and too much deference will keep you from seeing your boss clearly and realistically and prevent you from securing the work and personal benefits available from a good relationship.

What Should Your Relationship with Your Boss Be?

Do you realize that your relationship is actually one of *mutual* dependence? Your boss depends on you and needs your commitment and support to succeed. Just as you may wrestle with your reliance on your people, he probably struggles with his dependence on you and his other direct reports.

Think of the relationship as a partnership in which the partners depend on each other to succeed and are able to influence each other in ways that improve the performance of each. It's not a relationship of equals, certainly, but it's not entirely one-way either. You usually do have some room to negotiate and create the relationship that works for both of you.

Take Stock of Your Current Relationship

Is your current relationship a partnership? Are you and your boss able to have a normal, constructive discussion about work? If not, why not?

Don't assume you can make significant differences in how your boss thinks or operates. Most likely, the best you can do is nudge her in directions that work better for you. That's certainly worth doing. But you're unlikely to create large changes.

With that in mind, use the following questions to assess and improve your relationship. They focus on actions you can take.

Are you meeting expectations?

By far, the key factor in a good relationship is your ability to perform as expected.

Results. Performance targets create the foundation for your ongoing relationship. Unless you and your group produce the results expected, you're unlikely to enjoy much of a partnership. And it's not just the results you attain but *how* you attain them. If you hit your numbers but your boss hears complaints all day about how you railroad other groups, he probably won't consider you someone who "meets expectations."

Information. But results aren't the only expectation. Do you keep your boss informed? Reach explicit agreement about how often and in what way you will report progress. Develop a sense of what your boss wants to know. Some prefer to know a great deal; others, much less. In general, no boss likes to be surprised or seem ignorant of something she should know. If you must err, do it on the side of overinforming. Many bosses actually want more information than they say, so discover the right balance through experience. Find out as well how your boss wants information delivered: written reports via e-mail, in person if that's possible, or by video call.

Support and loyalty. Your goal is to make the relationship work for both of you, and that requires some degree of support and loyalty. Just as you want your boss to care about you, and your people want you to care about them, your boss wants your care and concern, too.

Be generous and assume the best intentions, even when you disagree. Express disagreement as your opinion offered in support of your boss's success. Some people bridle at the word *loyalty*. We don't mean blind loyalty, but loyal people earn the right to question and disagree on occasion. Those who speak up only when they disagree will usually enjoy less influence than those who have demonstrated prior support. So on those occasions when you do honestly agree with your boss, say so clearly and explicitly.

You cannot succeed in this relationship at the expense of your boss; you will rise or fall together. Your task is to make *both of you* effective. Help your boss build on her strengths, and overcome or bypass her limitations.

Does your boss trust you?

The foundation of all network relationships is trust, and the relationship with your boss is no different. Can he count on you to do the right thing? If you feel micromanaged, the reason may be that you've neglected to establish real trust. The essence of building trust is to negotiate what you both mean by "do the right thing."

Do you both see the current situation the same way? Make sure you share a common understanding of the challenges your group faces and what needs to be done. If you see the need for fundamental change and your boss wants to stay the course, you must resolve this difference right away.

Do you agree about where you and your group are going? Once again, a plan is critical. Do you have one? Have you reviewed it with your boss? Does it make clear what's to be done and when? Make sure your boss knows your goals and plans and agrees with them. Ideally, she had a hand in creating them.

Do you negotiate expectations when you're given an assignment? Don't let your relationship be one in which you simply accept whatever is passed down without discussion. If the expectations are unrealistic, you will have no one to blame but yourself when your team fails. Reach agreement on the results you're expected to produce—what will happen by when. Do this at the beginning, and update expectations periodically. Warn your boss of potential risks, and play out various scenarios of how you might handle them.

Do you see and understand your boss as a person?

It's easy to forget that beneath your boss's mantle of authority there's a person just like you. He has hopes, aspirations, frustrations, strengths, weaknesses, and fears. He's the product of his background, training, and experience. He has a personal life—a family and family history, religious beliefs, social organizations, political views, and hobbies. Do you know enough that you're able to see the world through his eyes?

Do you understand your boss as a manager?

Your boss has goals, plans, and pressures, as well as managerial strengths and weaknesses, preferences, and foibles. Do you know them? What's your boss on the line for? What's her boss telling her to do?

Do you know how your boss prefers to make decisions, and do you work within that pattern? Does he prefer lots of analysis and data? Does he need time to reach a conclusion? Does he want everyone's opinion before deciding? If you must depart from these preferences, do you first negotiate explicitly what you will do?

Do you know and respect the ways your boss prefers to work? Some bosses want written analyses before a discussion, while others prefer the discussion or presentation first, followed by a written summary. Some want lots of data; others want the highlights. Some want to be intimately involved in every detail; others prefer regular reports but nothing more unless there's a problem.

When you approach your boss, do you expect guidance or answers? We know a manager whose boss always responded to questions with questions of her own. Finally, this manager realized: "I had to come in with some ideas about how I would handle the situation, and then she would talk about them with me. She would spend all the time in the world with me."

Do you present a problem and expect your boss to solve it? Many bosses resist that approach. Instead, try going in with a problem, an analysis, alternatives, and a recommendation he can react to.

Can you identify your boss's strengths?

This stumps many managers we know. They focus on their boss's weaknesses and can talk at length about them—and often do with their peers. But they seldom look for strengths. That's a shame because your boss's strengths are what you must leverage, and you cannot leverage what you don't recognize or appreciate. Whatever your boss's weaknesses, identify what she does well. There must be something. Don't fall back on something like "She knows how to play the organizational game." There's something there. What is it, and how can you use it to learn and do your work more effectively?

Are you clear about what you need and expect?

Negotiate what you need from your boss. Don't make him guess. What can he do to help you? Provide resources, support from other groups, relief from distracting responsibilities, clearer direction?

In addition, think about the way you prefer to work and what you need from a superior, such as specific goals, help and ongoing guidance, or a certain degree of autonomy. Be sure you know where the boundaries are. Test how negotiable they are. Where your needs and your boss's way of managing diverge, talk through the differences. Where differences involve high stakes, talk sooner than later. It's easy to underestimate the risks of conflict avoidance and the cost of the passive aggression that often accompanies it. Your nonverbal communications—expression, manner, body language, tone—often reveal

CHECKLIST FOR MANAGING YOUR BOSS

Make sure you understand your boss and his or her context, including:

☐ Goals and objectives

☐ Pressures

☐ Strengths, weaknesses, blind spots

☐ Preferred work style

Assess yourself and your needs, including:

☐ Strengths and weaknesses

☐ Personal style

☐ Predisposition toward dependence on authority figures

Develop and maintain a relationship that:

☐ Fits both your needs and styles

☐ Is characterized by mutual expectations

☐ Keeps your boss informed

☐ Is based on dependability and honesty

☐ Selectively uses your boss's time and resources

Adapted from "Managing Your Boss" (product #R0501J) by John J. Gabarro and John P. Kotter, *Harvard Business Review*, January 2005 (republished from 1980) your true feelings about your boss and can slowly corrode this critical relationship.

Have you discussed with your boss your own growth, development, and aspirations?

How can your boss help you grow and develop? She's not responsible for your career and personal development, but it's in her best interest for you to improve in ways that will help you (and her) succeed. From your boss you can get advice and guidance; feedback about your performance, strengths, and weaknesses; insight into what others think of you; developmental assignments; and access to training programs and other learning opportunities.

To obtain these, you must first communicate your desire to learn. Then, you must agree about *how* and *where* you want to grow—what competencies you need to develop, such as building a network, making a plan, managing performance, or assessing subordinates. Have reasonable expectations. Take responsibility for your own development. Besides, your boss probably has no more time and no less pressure than you, and many bosses, unfortunately, are uncomfortable in this role. The more specific the requests you make, the better—to attend a training course, for example, or advice about a specific problem.

Do you and your boss come from different cultures?

Be aware that cultures differ in their expectations and treatment of people with authority. In some, the boss is expected to be participative; in others, directive. In some, proactive and assertive; in others, humble and modest.

Compare the characteristics of both your cultures. Where your assumptions and expectations differ, be prepared to talk about them explicitly.

Work hard to build a productive relationship with your boss. Initiate the kinds of discussions we've suggested. It's difficult to succeed without his support, and impossible in the face of his opposition. Always remember that your reports face these same issues with you. Let your experience in each relationship—with your boss and with your people—guide you in the other.

Don't make the mistake, as many managers do, of ignoring such a potentially powerful source of help and support. Take responsibility for, and play an active role in, making it a partnership that benefits both of you. Avoid seeing yourself as a passive, powerless subordinate. Don't assume it cannot be a positive, mutually helpful relationship until you've tested the possibilities on several occasions. It's too important—to your ability to exercise influence and thus to your journey—to merely let it be whatever it will be.

———

Linda A. Hill is the Wallace Brett Donham Professor of Business Administration and faculty chair of the Leadership Initiative at Harvard Business School. Now a writer and executive coach, **Kent Lineback** spent many years as a manager and an executive in business and government. They are the coauthors of *Being the Boss: The 3 Imperatives for Becoming a Great Leader* (Harvard Business Review Press, 2011).

Winning Over Your New Boss

by Lew McCreary

Getting a new boss can be fraught with anxiety and risk, often making it hard to see the opportunities fresh leadership will bring to you and your organization. You'll have to come to terms with whatever unpredictable changes she unleashes. Don't expect the new regime to resemble the old one. Leaders are often brought in to shake up the status quo, so you'll want to make it clear right away that you're a valuable contributor.

If you get a new boss by joining another organization, you'll have no immediate worries about job security. But you will need to figure out the culture (and its politics), meet with and impress new colleagues and direct reports, and above all create a successful partnership with your new boss. You'll need to understand—quickly and in detail—exactly what you've been brought aboard to do, what key stakeholders you'll need to please, what resources you can command, and how your performance in the job will be measured.

In either new-boss scenario, uncertainties abound—but you have a role to play in taming them. As Tom Gilmore, a principal at the Center for Applied Research (CFAR), points out, you're just as responsible as your new boss for "the quality of the working alliance."

What does that responsibility involve? Establishing yourself as someone the new boss can turn to for candid opinions, insight, and support—someone she can count on to perform. Here are some tips for doing that.

Prepare to Meet the New Boss

Because your first meeting with your new boss feels like a make-or-break encounter—especially if she's the one who's new to the company and presumably looking for things to change—you may be tempted to lead with your personal agenda. If you do, you'll be part of a steady parade of petitioners, each bearing (as the leader sees it) a narrow set of demands.

Don't arrive at that initial meeting with thick stacks of documents and a PowerPoint presentation. And don't prepare an eager audition that recapitulates your LinkedIn recommendations. Instead, ask questions and listen to the answers. Find out who the new boss is, how she likes to work, what she doesn't yet know that you can help her learn. Answer her questions candidly as well, and don't be so tightly clenched that you fail to let the boss see who you are.

Gilmore, drawing on his experience and research at CFAR, offers the following advice for making crucial early encounters successful:

- **Ease into the relationship.** Think incrementally. Pick only a few vital issues to cover early on— ones that will help you lay the groundwork for an effective alliance with your new boss. For instance, initially brief her on your unit's new open-innovation initiatives. Over time, you can discuss in more depth the projects that have been green-lighted so far.

- **Observe her style.** Does your new boss prefer short or long conversations? A buffet of options or one best recommendation? Hard data or soft? Use these indicators to shape the way you present yourself and your ideas.

- **Consider others' claims on her attention.** It may be just the two of you sitting in her office, but you're not the only one who wants something from her. Take account of how other key stakeholders might affect her agenda, and highlight how your issues fit into those overall priorities.

- **Collaborate.** Help her form opinions on issues of importance to you, her, and the group. Avoid simply seeking her judgment on your ideas. If, for example, you believe the group has grown too risk-averse, begin a broader discussion about risk. Share anecdotes about how the group has dealt with it in the past, and ask about her experiences and ideas.

- **Be honest.** Most leaders understand the difficulty of speaking truth to power, and yet they must depend at first on relative strangers for honest appraisals. Look for openings to provide helpful candor on some key aspect of the new boss's agenda. Say your boss wants to launch an initiative that would require buy-in from two unit heads who don't work well together. Diplomatically bring that dynamic to her attention and share stories of how others have been able to get the two to cooperate.

- **Accommodate her preferences.** Your new boss has inherited systems and processes tailored to her predecessor's quirks. The more you can learn about how she would like to be supported, the faster you can help develop new systems that work for her. For example, if her style is to delegate, suggest a regular weekly meeting to review assignments and workloads. Let her know what sorts of tasks you're best suited to take on and keep her apprised of your bandwidth.

Establish a sense of connection, says Gilmore, by "finding links between what you'd like to see happen and things the new boss wants to accomplish." There will be time for your agenda after you've built a solid relationship.

Be Yourself and Be Transparent

J. Bruce Harreld, who now teaches at Harvard Business School, has both been a new boss and reported to one many times—at IBM, Boston Chicken, Kraft General Foods, and elsewhere.

Whether you're getting a new boss at your current company or joining a different one, Harreld says, "The best advice I can give . . . is just to be yourself and be transparent. The more I think about 'What should I say to the boss?' the more he and I are both in trouble. I'm there for a reason—for my best opinion. And he's there for a reason, which is to guide me and help me learn, and shape what my work agenda should be. And the more I posture to him, the less effective I am." In effect, it lowers the value of the relationship.

Candor goes hand in glove with confidentiality. Don't share your boss's comments with others unless he's asked you to. And beware of carrying tales of your peers back to him. "A lot of people view their boss as someone they have to tell everything to," says Harreld. "You have to be careful with that. In a complex organization, if you view the CEO as the kingmaker, you're putting yourself at risk. If I wear my power with my boss on my sleeve, and people know I run back to him often, I've just cut out all these other relationships and made myself totally ineffective."

When Harreld worked for Lou Gerstner at IBM in the mid-1990s, they didn't always agree, but they never pulled their punches: "That's part of the process, part of being on a team. You make your recommendation as forcefully as you can. And once the decision is made, you have to snap around and say, 'OK, here we go.' And sometimes people can't [make that pivot]—they get strident. And sometimes they have to leave the team."

That's worth remembering. The agenda for change may stretch farther than you and others are willing to go. Many new leaders have transformational marching orders. Your job in the course of a leadership transition is to see how compatible the new boss's plans are with your own agenda and career goals. If they're at odds, you might have some thinking to do. And, of course, that thinking cuts both ways: If you're on the edge of disillusionment, a new boss can be a breath of fresh air, helping to rekindle your enthusiasm and optimism.

Help Your New Boss Get Up to Speed

If she's new to the organization, your boss has a lot of catching up to do. You can make it easier by:

- **Saving her some time.** Be generous with what and whom you know. Help your boss identify colleagues whose expertise will help her meet her goals.

- **Saving her some trouble.** Share shortcuts through the administrative mazes that drive every newbie crazy. This may seem like a small thing, but it's not. Let her know that Phil in the IT user-services group is the only person to call when her technology goes on the fritz. Or that Maureen in Finance has developed an idiot-proof Excel template for expense reports.

- **Saving her some work.** Being new is a job unto itself. There may be something on the boss's plate that you can take on or at least help with. If you see an opportunity, step up. Suppose your boss has been asked to honor her predecessor's speaking commitment at an industry conference, and it's clear she's not happy about going. Since you know your way around the presentation material, volunteer to fill in.

Listen for Clues to the Future

In town-hall get-acquainted sessions, new bosses often default to being politic and careful. Sometimes, however, telling comments slip out. File these away as possible clues to the mysterious future. Some of them will doubtless be worth probing later when you have one-on-one meetings with the boss.

Also bear in mind that you may end up with a new boss who isn't right for the business. Pay close attention to what she says (and how she says it). You may be able to spot trouble brewing early on. A former colleague and I, in our first joint meeting with a new boss, were surprised to hear him say, contentedly, that he really had "nothing to prove." Since just about everyone in the company was energetically focused on proving something, the comment seemed discordant. In less than a year, the new boss and the company parted ways.

Remember That the Stakes Are High

Reuben Slone has weathered—and learned from—numerous new-boss transitions in his career. He recently left OfficeMax, where he was an executive VP leading the supply-chain organization, for a comparable position at Walgreens. While at OfficeMax, he had five bosses in eight years.

Each time he's had to adapt to a new boss, Slone has reread the *Harvard Business Review* article "Surviving Your New CEO" (May 2007). He dusted it off again as he prepared for his new assignment at Walgreens, where his challenge is to take an increasingly complicated supply chain—with a growing set of channels, customers, and offerings—to the next level of sophistication.

Slone values the article's tips on how to build a strong relationship with your new leader, whether it's you or your boss who's joining the organization. But he also re-reads it for a reality check: It includes sobering research on the jeopardy executives face when a new boss takes over. In some cases, turnover among top executives is 33%—nearly double the normal rate. So every opportunity to make an impression matters tremendously.

Slone's advice? "Make sure the boss knows he can count on you, what he can count on you for, and that you're there to help make the transition as easy as possible. Be explicit about that. And get in early—don't wait for him to come to you."

———————

Lew McCreary is an editorial consultant and a contributing editor to HBR. Working as a consultant means he gets new bosses regularly. He has learned that the most valuable attribute is to be flexible—up to a point.

Steps for Presenting Problems or Opportunities to Your Boss

Did your project come in $10,000 over budget? A rival poach your star performer? Your competitor beat you to market with a new product? None of us likes to deliver a difficult message, but it can be a valuable tool for building a trusting relationship with your boss. You know that you should never bring a problem to your boss without a proposed solution. But often we forget to frame the situation in a way that helps us garner the necessary resources or approval to begin moving toward a solution.

Adapted from *Managing Up* (product #14784) from the Pocket Mentor series, Harvard Business Review Press, 2008

Here are five steps to take the next time you need to deliver bad news—or a promising opportunity.

1. **Describe the problem or opportunity to your boss.** Provide a general overview of the problem, and show the specific impact it has on your work and the company's goals. If you've identified an opportunity, show the potential benefits—not just to you or your team, but to the larger organization.

   "Stu, we've got a morale problem on our tech team. Our recent employee survey shows that 40% of our staff in Atlanta doesn't find their work rewarding or challenging. If we don't address this, we might lose some of our best talent. We can't afford that at any time, but especially now when we're trying to release the new system by Q1. I have a few ideas I'd like to try, with your help and the cooperation of HR. I think with the right approach we can keep the team focused on meeting the Q1 goal."

2. **Identify your solution or approach.** Explain how you've already tried to solve the problem and what you've learned from those attempts. Recommend a specific approach, along with alternatives, to provide your manager with options.

   Clearly define each possible option, addressing the pros and cons, and any potential risks or barriers. Explain the logic behind your recommended approach. You want your manager to be aware that you've considered several possible outcomes.

"It looks like we'd need to add two more managers to the project to meet the client's latest round of requests. When I mentioned this to Sarah during our conference call, she didn't respond. I'd like to go to Cincinnati and meet with her to discuss how we might renegotiate the contract. I think seeing her face-to-face will make a big difference. Plus if I do it the week after next, we'll have just delivered on the second phase of the project and she's likely to be pleased. We could of course take the hard line and just say no to their requests and then see what they come back with. But I'm afraid we'd be putting our future relationship at risk. We could also just expand the team and do the work and see it as a marketing investment. We'd likely win Sarah's good graces and, as you know, she's well connected with many companies in our target group. But it may be more financial risk than we're willing to take on right now."

3. **Explain the implications.** Consider the impact that your proposed solution will have on yourself and others, including your manager. Be explicit about how your idea will have far-reaching effects on the goals of the organization.

   "If we put a formal process in place to track all sales leads, I can do a better job of connecting the dots between the VPs who are meeting with potential customers. As you know, the current approach worked well when we just had two VPs doing the calls, but now we have over 20. This will increase their workload slightly, but it will be clearer to them how to share lead information. It will also give senior leadership a better view into the pipeline. It won't take a week to pull together our sales dev reports, which means you can be more responsive to requests from above."

4. **Discuss the benefits.** Focus your conversation on concrete examples of your idea's benefits. The specific features of the solution, or how it will be implemented, are less important at this stage. If you have tested your approach on a small scale with good results, share that information.

"Delivering the product in a smaller container in the Latin American market will expand our customer base. We'll be able to serve truckers with small rigs who go on long hauls but don't have room for the 20-gallon containers. Most of these truckers haven't bought our products before, so we have the opportunity to convert them to our brand. They'll also be able to pay cash, since the smaller container will be at a lower price point. This is a real advantage in their cash-heavy economy. Carlos helped me run a quick experiment with a small set of truckers in Panama, and the response was overwhelmingly positive."

5. **Accept responsibility for the outcome.** Demonstrate your commitment to ensuring success. Work with your manager to develop a final action plan for taking advantage of the opportunity you've presented.

"This rests squarely on my shoulders. In the unlikely event that we don't convert enough customers from this campaign, I'll quickly move on to Plan B. But to get started I'm going to reach out to Terry to get the e-mail list of current customers who have opted-in. Then I'll work with Ellen to draft the e-mail pitch. Once I've done that, I'd like to get your help running it up the flagpole. Does that sound like a sensible plan to you?"

Manage Up with Your Mentor's Guidance

by Jeanne C. Meister

Your mentors can help you build better relationships with your boss and colleagues. How? Jeanne Meister, an expert in workplace learning and development, recently shared her ideas in an IdeaCast interview with Susan Francis from HBR. Here are some highlights.

What kind of support can mentors offer as you're trying to manage up?

Mentors can help you navigate your company's political landscape and introduce you to key people so you can branch out. And they'll get you thinking like a senior executive long before you're anointed as a member of the upper ranks—which will prepare you for that metamorphosis. One of my first mentors shared this valuable advice with me: Know who the thought leaders are across the organization, get to know them personally, and show them how your ideas can further their business agendas.

Mentors can also help you communicate your ideas to senior executives, who juggle myriad demands and don't have time to wade through a sea of PowerPoint slides. If you want to present a complex idea to a group like this, take a first pass at boiling it down to a one-page memo that focuses on business outcomes. Then turn to one of your mentors for input: Have you crafted a message that will get executives' attention—one that clearly and succinctly shows how your idea will affect the bottom line? What details should you trim? Where do you need to add data for support?

How can mentors help you work more effectively with your boss?

They can provide insight into the high-level challenges your boss faces and suggest realistic ways of supporting his goals. Ask your boss to clarify his top priorities with you—and write up a one- or two-page summary of that conversation to share with a trusted mentor. Then think with your mentor about how you can contribute. Maybe you can volunteer to assemble sales data your boss will need for his big presentation to the executive board, for example, or tap your network to gather anecdotal feedback on a product idea he's considering.

Also try asking a mentor for help processing and incorporating feedback from your boss. Suppose you've been told you need to speak up more in large staff meetings, but you're shy. You and a mentor can practice graceful ways of jumping into the conversation or brainstorm other things you can do to show you're engaged.

Part of managing up is figuring out which organizational battles to fight and how to fight them. What can mentors do to make this easier?

They can help you develop your personal brand—which will make it clearer which battles you should take on. For instance, if you want to be known at your company for your creative product ideas, a mentor can broker opportunities for you to present them. She'll also help you develop a better sense of when to go to the mat over them. For example, you and your mentor may decide it's worth fighting to protect your vision for a new product's positioning, but not to control the timing of its introduction.

Making sure your mentor gets value out of working with you is obviously good practice for managing up. Any suggestions on how?

This is almost the same as understanding your boss's priorities. When you know what's important to her, you can find ways to work toward her objectives. Simple gestures go a long way—for instance, putting her top three subjects of interest in your Google alerts and passing along links you think she'll like. Look at her Twitter feed for insights into what she cares about: What kinds of conversations is she having— and how can you participate? Ask your mentor about her personal goals and see how you can help her achieve them. Suppose she's writing an article on pricing strategy for a marketing journal. Offer to read the manuscript and provide feedback from an execution perspective. If you find ways to give as well as receive, your mentor will take note—and become all the more invested in your development.

Jeanne C. Meister is a partner at Future Workplace, which helps organizations redefine their corporate learning and talent management strategies. She is a coauthor, with Karie Willyerd, of *The 2020 Workplace: How Innovative Companies Attract, Develop, and Keep Tomorrow's Employees Today* (HarperBusiness, 2010).

Change the Way You Persuade

A summary of the full-length HBR article by **Gary A. Williams** *and* **Robert B. Miller,** *highlighting key ideas.*

THE IDEA IN BRIEF

Your proposal was brilliant; your logic, unassailable; your argument, impassioned. So why didn't your boss buy it?

Perhaps you took a one-size-fits-all approach to persuasion. But different people use different styles when deciding to accept an idea: Each wants certain kinds of information, at specific steps in the process.

There are five common but distinct decision-making styles: charismatic, thinker, skeptic, follower, and controller. One decision-making style isn't better than another. But to tip the outcome your way, understand your listener's preferences—then tailor your persuasive efforts accordingly.

Reprint #R0205D

THE IDEA IN PRACTICE

Style	Decision-Maker's Characteristics	Prominent Examples	Persuader's Strategy	Examples of How to Approach Them
Charismatic	• Easily enthralled, but bases decisions on balanced information • Emphasizes bottom-line results	• Lee Iacocca • Herb Kelleher	• Focus on results • Make straightforward arguments • Stress proposal's benefits with visual aids	• Diagram your current organization and the problem(s), proposed solution(s), and benefits—especially improved competitiveness • Explain potential challenges and risk of inaction • Provide detailed reports for your boss to review postpresentation
Thinker	• Toughest to persuade • Cerebral, logical • Risk-averse • Needs extensive detail	• Michael Dell • Bill Gates	• Present market research, customer surveys, case studies, cost/benefit analyses • Help your boss understand all perspectives of a given situation	• Present different options in detail in a face-to-face meeting • Explain your data-gathering methods • Present case studies of similar initiatives • Use a follow-up meeting to fill argument gaps and recommend optimum plan • Wait weeks, months for your boss's decision
Skeptic	• Challenges every data point • Decides based on gut feelings	• Larry Ellison • Tom Siebel	• Establish credibility ahead of time with your expertise; draw on positive previous work experiences • Get endorsements from someone your boss trusts	• Copresent with a trusted colleague • Emphasize the credibility of your sources of information • Stroke your boss's ego ("You've probably seen this case study...") • Ground your argument in the real world

Follower	• Relies on own or others' past decisions to make current choices • Late adopter	• Carly Fiorina • Peter Coors	• Use testimonials to prove low risk • Present innovative, yet proven, solutions	• Highlight case studies from other industries, but note "We could be the first in our industry to do this." • Omit failed real-world examples (although you should have this information available should your boss request it) • Present multiple options • Tap your network for references to steer your boss toward your preferred choice; emphasize the option's affordability, etc.
Controller	• Unemotional, analytical • Abhors uncertainty • Implements only own ideas	• Martha Stewart • Ross Perot	• Present highly structured arguments • Make your boss "own" the data • Avoid aggressive advocacy	• Over several months, send your boss customer reports, marketing studies, financial projections; give him everything he needs to build your case for you • Emphasize data highlighting the company's challenge • Identify data contradictions, but let your boss analyze them • Wait for your boss to request a meeting after a significant incident (e.g., a large customer defects)

Gary A. Williams is the CEO of Miller-Williams Incorporated, a San Diego–based customer research firm. He can be reached at gaw@millwill.com. **Robert B. Miller** is the chairman of Miller-Williams Incorporated. He is the co-author of several business books, including *Strategic Selling*. He can be reached at rbm@millwill.com.

Get to Know Your Boss's Boss

by Priscilla Claman

Does your boss's boss know you well? Is she impressed with you? Does she know exactly what you do? If you can't answer these questions with a "yes," you're missing out on career opportunities.

Here's a person with a broad perspective on your organization, someone who can see what's coming down the pike—whether it's a new product or a reorg—more clearly than you or your boss can. Forming a relationship with her will help you develop a 30,000-foot view, too. But it's more than that. She has a direct say in your growth and advancement. She approves your performance reviews, raises, promotions, and major changes in duties. She also signs off on any professional development you might be offered, such as stretch assignments or formal training.

Adapted from content posted on hbr.org on November 17, 2011

To succeed in your organization, you need her to know your skills and have an idea of what your career plans are. Yes, your own boss is supposed to advocate for you, but he still has to get the approval of his boss. When you and others are competing for a promotion, it will go to someone your boss's boss thinks highly of.

But how do you get to know her? How do you earn her attention and respect? Here are some suggestions:

- **Interact with her.** It sounds basic, but smile and say "hello" when you see her. Some people duck and run when a powerful person comes into their work area. Instead, ask how you can help her. Re-introduce yourself if you see she doesn't remember you. Treat her like the very important customer she is.

- **Reach out to her.** Touch base when opportunities arise. If she gets a promotion or award, send her a congratulatory e-mail. If you find an article or book that's relevant to her interests, send her a link and ask whether she's heard about it.

- **Tap her for advice.** E-mail her to ask for input on courses you're thinking of taking, professional organizations you're considering joining, and more. First make sure it's OK with your boss, though, and use his name in your message so it's clear you're not bypassing the chain of command. Suppose your boss has asked you to research some new vendors, and you know his boss has several strong candidates in her extensive network. Send her your list of finalists to see if she has any experience with them or knows of other good options. And when you do this, make your boss look good. Preface your question with, "John thought you might have some helpful insights for us . . ." Follow up on her suggestions and thank her for them when you write to let her know which vendor you've chosen and why.

- **Extend an invitation.** Do you have an interesting guest coming in for a meeting? Are you giving a presentation? Is your manager leading a training session? Ask your boss if you should invite his boss. Whether she comes or not, it's another chance to let them both know that you're thinking of the big picture.

- **Pass along praise.** Forward complimentary e-mails from colleagues or customers to your boss. He'll most likely send them on to his boss, since your success reflects well on him, too. Customer compliments are highly regarded, whether the customers are internal or external.

- **Volunteer for a cross-functional team.** Leading or joining a cross-functional team is a great way to contribute to the larger organization. So is offering to take notes at meetings and circulate them afterward. Most people see this as drudgery, but it's an opportunity to raise your visibility. Ask team members if they'd like you to copy their managers, and see if your boss would like you to copy his boss. If they say yes, your notes—and your name—will be noticed by the senior team, including your boss's boss.

- **Fix a problem.** If you find a way to make an improvement that furthers a business objective or supports a corporate value, act on it—and share the results with your boss's boss. Here's an example: An administrative assistant at a global nonprofit found her organization's customer-tracking system inaccurate and hard to use. When she discovered that many colleagues felt the same way, she researched other systems. Some friends in accounting pulled together a cost/benefit analysis for her so she could develop a proposal for switching to a new system, which she presented to her boss and her boss's boss. She not only got funding for the project, she also earned a new leadership role: overseeing the conversion and managing the new system.

Try these tips, and your boss's boss will know—and care—who you are.

Priscilla Claman is president of Career Strategies, a Boston-based firm offering career coaching to individuals and competency development and career management services to organizations.

How to Make Your Boss Look Good— Without Becoming a Sycophant

by Michael Schrage

I find suck-ups loathsome. But I admire the managing-up technique I've seen ambitious people skillfully deploy. No fawning or flattery—they make smart use of technology to make their bosses look good.

For example, the boss's boss at one marketing firm had given a keynote speech at a major industry event. A twentysomething analyst easily found a couple of complimentary tweets referencing the talk. He e-mailed them to his fortysomething boss, who barely knew what Twitter was, but who was thrilled to bring them to his

---

Adapted from content posted on hbr.org on April 15, 2010

boss's attention. Win. Win. Win. Everyone was happy. A simple 90-second investment made his boss look good.

At another firm, a project manager found that her boss's boss had an offbeat sense of humor and liked injecting levity into boring project reviews. She made it her mission to find the appropriate *New Yorker* or Dilbert cartoon to paste into a PowerPoint slide for presentations. Of course, she didn't do this for her own presentations; she selected amusing and relevant options for her boss's talk. He was grateful, and the boss's boss liked them.

What I like about making your boss look good is that it is the mirror image of the marketing mantra about knowing the customer's customer. Understanding your boss is vital. But researching, knowing, and appreciating your boss's boss ought to give you valuable insight into what makes your boss effective—and frustrated. That shapes how to better position your boss in the mind of *his* boss.

Your Boss as a Brand

If you saw your boss as a brand, how would you sell that brand to the ultimate customer—your boss's boss? Answering this question well requires market research. What can you do that will move your project forward and make your boss look good to his boss and peers, too? It can be a worthwhile investment of your time to consider what tools and technologies may help you.

The economic and technological "barriers of entry" to figuring out appropriate approaches to making your boss look good have collapsed. Most managers are but a LinkedIn connection or a blog comment away from insights into their boss's boss that makes a win-win-win outcome a good bet. Should this occur daily? Only if you're comfortable being the teacher's pet. But there's nothing wrong with making your boss look good be a part of *your* brand.

Perhaps you think it would test the outer limits of your creativity and authenticity to make your boss look good. But give it a try. Think of it as a marketing challenge: What are the two things you could do in the next three days that would make your boss look better to his boss?

––––––––––––––

Michael Schrage, a research fellow at MIT Sloan School's Center for Digital Business, is the author of *Serious Play* (Harvard Business School Press, 1999) and the forthcoming *Getting Beyond Ideas.*

Stop Being Micromanaged

by Amy Gallo

None of us likes a boss who constantly scrutinizes our work. Micromanagers are not only annoying, their lack of faith may make you doubt yourself and stunt your professional growth. But you don't have to suffer with an overly controlling boss. If you reduce your micromanager's stress, you may be able to secure the autonomy you need.

What the Experts Say

Micromanagement can make you feel inept, but typically it has nothing to do with your performance. "It's more about your boss's level of internal anxiety and need to control situations than anything about you," says Jenny Chatman, a professor of management at Haas School of Business at UC Berkeley.

Adapted from content posted on hbr.org on September 22, 2011

You can't change the way your boss leads, but you can change the way you follow using these tactics:

Evaluate Your Boss's Behavior

Jean-François Manzoni, coauthor of *The Set-Up-to-Fail Syndrome: How Good Managers Cause Great People to Fail*, cautions that all controlling bosses are not the same. On one end of the spectrum are managers with very high standards. They may regularly have you rework something that doesn't measure up. They pay a great deal of attention to detail and exercise some degree of control, but they don't stifle you. In fact, you may learn a lot from them.

At the other end of the spectrum are people Manzoni describes as "pathological micromanagers who need to make it clear to themselves and others that they are in charge." These are the bosses who give you little to no independence, insist on being involved in every detail of your work, and are more concerned about specifics, such as font size, than the big picture. "You know you're working with [a pathological micromanager] if he gets involved in a level of detail that is way below his pay grade," says Chatman.

Don't Fight It

Railing against micromanagement isn't productive. "If you push back in one way or another—passively or aggressively—your manager may conclude you can't be trusted and get more involved," says Manzoni. It may be tempting to complain, but it will probably only make your situation worse. "If I sense disdain, I'm going to be encouraged to show you that on my forehead it says 'boss' and on yours, it doesn't," says Manzoni. Instead, try to understand what's causing your boss's behavior. Is he under immense pressure? Is this his intuitive way of managing? Does the company culture encourage and reward this kind of behavior? If you recognize the underlying reasons, you can figure out how to respond.

Increase Trust

Micromanagement is usually "based on a general view that the world's standards are not up to what they should be," says Chatman. You therefore need to make a conscious effort to earn your manager's trust by succeeding in the dimensions that he cares most about. "You absolutely, positively must deliver and deliver in a way that doesn't increase your boss's stress. In fact, identify things that reduce [it]," says Manzoni. If you meet your boss's standards—deliver work on time, make sure projects include the elements she wants—she's likely to see you as someone she can lean on. The more she trusts you, the less inclined she'll be to tell you exactly how to do something.

Make Up-front Agreements

Another tactic is to talk to your boss—before a project starts—about how he'll be involved. "Try to agree on standards and basic approach," says Manzoni. What role will each of you play? What criteria will you use to measure the project's success? Explain what you think the ideal plan of action is and then ask for his input. "Be sure you understand up front what the guiding principles are for the work—not just the tactical elements," says Chatman. For example, if you're working on an internal marketing campaign, be sure to talk about the message you want to send, not the font you should use. If the discussion becomes overly focused on detail, try to bring it back to the principles and approach you agreed on. Flattery can also work. Remind your boss that he's better off not getting involved in the minutiae because his time and effort are more valuable to the big picture.

Keep Your Boss in the Loop

Remember that micromanagers are often motivated by anxiety. "They are nervous about anyone else being able to do things as well or in the same way they would," says Chatman. Address that concern by keeping your manager informed of your project's progress. Schedule regular check-ins to help her feel part of the process. Or send unprompted e-mails that share important information. If she wants detail, get specific. Although annoying now, it may save you the effort of redoing work later on.

Give Feedback, but Only if Appropriate

Telling a micromanager that you don't appreciate his controlling behavior may only trigger more of it. But some managers may be open to hearing your input. "Try to catch your boss in a moment of openness," says Manzoni. He suggests using the time in a scheduled performance review. Focus your feedback on how his behavior affects the process. Can you tweak his involvement so that he gets the information he needs without becoming a roadblock?

Get Help or Move On

If none of these approaches work for you, ask yourself: Do I really want to work here? "If it's pathological, you should consider transferring to another part of the company or finding another job," says Manzoni. Before you throw in the towel, however, look to others inside the company. Find a trusted coworker or a reliable HR manager who can counsel you. At the very least, you'll be able to do some restorative venting, and you may uncover additional tactics that could work for you.

Principles to Remember

- Do everything you can to gain the micromanager's trust

- Know what worries your boss and try to reduce her concerns

- Provide regular and detailed updates so your boss is aware of your progress

- Don't defy the micromanager—that often triggers more of the behavior you're trying to avoid

Case Study:
Be Attentive to Her Concerns

In 2006, Marcy Berke (names have been changed) worked for an insurance company with offices throughout the U.S. Her boss's boss was a woman named Barbara, who was responsible for 10 agencies in her region. Barbara was passionate about efficiency. She asked all the agents in her region to produce a time report, accounting for the number of minutes each of them spent on various tasks each day. "She was concerned with keeping her own production figures up and burnishing her image with senior management," Marcy says.

Marcy recognized what mattered most to Barbara. "If I were heading up a project, I would make certain to e-mail Barbara, early and often, with any questions I might have about what her expectations were, and give her an outline of what my team was working on and the anticipated date of completion," she says. If her team was having difficulty meeting the deadline for any reason, she would let Barbara know as soon as possible, providing both a reason and a revised end date. Marcy supplied the information Barbara needed without being asked first so that Barbara could learn to trust her.

Since Marcy knew that Barbara was so preoccupied with time, she arrived at least two or three minutes early for meetings. When Marcy needed to set up a meeting with Barbara, she would make the request by e-mail, clearly stating the reason for the meeting, listing the questions she would be asking, and indicating how long the meeting would last.

This approach worked well for Marcy. She was able to thrive at the company for four years, despite Barbara's micromanagement, before she left to start her own firm.

———————

Amy Gallo is a contributing editor at *Harvard Business Review*. Follow her on Twitter at @amyegallo.

Dealing with Your Incompetent Boss

by Amy Gallo

We all complain about our bosses from time to time. Some of us even consider it part of our job descriptions. But there's a difference between watercooler griping and paralyzing frustration, just as there's a clear distinction between a manager with a few flaws and one who is truly incompetent. So how can you handle your bad boss?

What the Experts Say

"Most people have had experience with someone who is incompetent, or at least unhelpful," says Annie McKee, coauthor of *Becoming a Resonant Leader: Develop Your Emotional Intelligence, Renew Your Relationships, Sustain Your Effectiveness*. That's because too many companies promote people for the wrong reasons. Whether

---

Adapted from content posted on hbr.org on June 6, 2011

your boss lacks technical or managerial ability, says Michael Useem, author of *Leading Up*, bad bosses sap motivation, kill productivity, and can make you want to run from the job screaming.

Although leaving is sometimes an option, it's not the only one for coping with a bad boss. Consider these tactics first:

Understand Your Boss's Incompetence

Before you declare your boss useless, check your bias and better understand what you're seeing. "When you're looking at your boss, the first thing you need to do before you judge is look at yourself," says McKee. Many of us have blind spots when it comes to our bosses. Ask yourself if you're jealous of her position in the organization or if you have a natural tendency to resist authority.

Also ". . . be cautious about your judgment until you collect all the evidence," says Useem. Your boss may have stressors you don't see or fully understand. "It's very common for people to completely miss the pressures their bosses are under; partly because a good manager will buffer you from them," says McKee. By learning about your boss and developing empathy for him, you may reevaluate his competence. Even if you still conclude that he's incapable, remember that he's human. Don't demonize him.

Ask Others for Help

Look to peers or people outside the organization for advice and a place to vent. This doesn't mean indiscriminate moaning about your boss. Instead find confidants: a trusted colleague, a spouse, a mentor, or a coach. Explain what you're seeing, how it's affecting you and your work, and ask for advice. "This is not to conspire against your boss but to check your point of view," says Useem. People outside the situation can give you a fresh perspective or offer new coping strategies.

Find a Way to Make It Work

Regardless of your boss's incompetence, you need to work together to get your job done. Be creative in collaborating with her. Figure out where she excels and then find ways to pair your strengths with her weaknesses. For example, if your boss is a competent writer but falls apart in front of an audience, suggest ways you can help with her presentation to the executive team. Can you listen to her trial run? Or present portions of it, as a development opportunity for you?

When you request something from her—whether it's input on a work plan, an introduction to a colleague, or her permission to reach out to a client—be specific about what you need. And do as much of the work for her as you can: Provide a draft e-mail or point out the three areas you'd like her to comment on. If she's unable to help, suggest an alternative: Perhaps you can ask one of her peers or superiors for input or the introduction. Your goal is to help her solve the problem, not set up more situations where she'll fail.

Step Up

Rather than give up on an ineffectual boss, focus on what *you* can do to make up the difference. If your boss fails to set priorities for the team, propose some that he can then approve or tweak. If meeting follow-up isn't his strength, offer to send out the to-dos. Without harboring resentment, do what's best for your team and the organization. Recognize that stepping up can be a growth opportunity; you may be taking on responsibilities someone at your level doesn't usually have. And in the process, you gain the respect and appreciation of other higher-ups.

Develop Yourself

Sometimes incompetence can manifest itself in a lack of communication. You may have a manager who hasn't given you a clear sense of your goals or even a concrete job description. These are essential to doing your job well and advancing your career, so take them on yourself. Write your own job description and articulate goals for the quarter or year. Send them to your boss and ask to review them together. In person, you can then confirm your priorities and understand her expectations. If she's still unresponsive, keep a record of what you've proposed and work to meet the goals you laid out. It may be that she isn't sure what you should be working on and needs you to just take action.

Take Care of Yourself

Working for an incompetent boss can be bad for your health. "There's a lot of research on the negative psychological effects," says McKee. She suggests creating boundaries that protect you from the emotional damage. We have a tendency to point to a bad boss and say, "He's ruining my life." But this ignores the fact that you have agency in the situation. "Once you become a victim, you cease to become a leader," she says. Focus on what makes you happy about your job, not miserable. "We can come to work every day and pay attention to this horrible boss, or we can choose to pay attention to the people we are happy to see every day and the work we enjoy. We can choose which emotions we lean into," says McKee.

Whenever possible, take on projects that allow you to spend time in other parts of the organization or with other leaders. Identify a mentor who can provide you with the feedback and instruction you aren't getting from your boss. Find a way to let off steam, such as taking short breaks throughout the day. Look for humor in the situation, and try not to allow one person to ruin your day, your job, or your career.

———————

Amy Gallo is a contributing editor at *Harvard Business Review*. Follow her on Twitter at @amyegallo.

Coping with a Conflict-Averse Boss

by Anne Field

Does your boss avoid conflict at any cost? Do you find it difficult to get the resources you need because your boss won't advocate for you? Does she push your team to the brink because she fears saying no to requests from above?

Here's how to cope—and get the critical feedback and guidance you need.

Make Conflict More Comfortable

Having a defensive and conflict-averse boss doesn't mean you can never disagree with him. When an issue crops up, frame it in terms that will get the best results *for your business*. Play devil's advocate. Ask lots of "what if?" questions. "What if our printer continues to have quality-control issues? Might it be a good idea to start

Adapted from reprint #C0504A

investigating other options now just in case?" Use gentle lead-ins such as "I might be off base here, but . . ." or "This might sound like a crazy idea, but . . ." all the while reassuring your boss that you're working toward the same goal as he is.

Focus on Problem Solving

If you need to talk about a difficult issue with your boss, focus on the problem, not the people. This will help establish neutral ground.

Offer specific suggestions. For example, if your weekly team meeting has turned into a gripe session for your colleagues, volunteer to create and distribute agendas. "I know how busy you are preparing the Williams presentation, so why don't I poll everyone for agenda items for this week's meeting?" You'll help provide a structure for your boss to approve and then follow.

Gather Supporting Evidence

If you want your boss to use her authority on your behalf, give her everything she needs to build her case: assemble data, write drafts, zero in on how your request fits into larger unit or organizational goals.

For example, a manager in a consumer products company dragged her feet when her staff urged her to ask for a bigger budget. So, they gathered the necessary backup, specifying each team member's duties, and the resources needed to meet their goals. They highlighted how meeting their goals would contribute to the unit's overall strategy. With that ammunition in hand, the boss approached senior management with greater confidence.

Put It in Writing

If your boss dreads face-to-face conversations, especially performance reviews, send him e-mails and brief documents outlining your key accomplishments and areas of development. This will make it easier for him to engage in a productive conversation with you—rather than coming up with the documentation on his own.

Guidelines can also help your conflict-averse boss work with larger groups. If his glossing over disagreements inhibits your team's ability to air differences, check your perception with your teammates offline. If they also feel that he's squelching productive debates in favor of peaceful chats, raise the issue with your boss in a one-on-one meeting. Propose that a little debate might help stoke the team's creativity and that setting ground rules for such discussions would ensure that they're productive. Volunteer to take notes to help keep the creative ideas moving along to implementation.

Ease In

If you know that your boss will find a conversation awkward or unpleasant, don't rush into it. Instead, open with a neutral, nonthreatening icebreaker. Cite a recent newspaper article about a common interest. Ask about her child or pet. Once you sense that she's comfortable, ease into the discussion.

Anne Field is a business writer based in Pelham, New York.

How to Give Your Boss Feedback

by Amy Gallo

Have you ever wished you could tell your boss exactly what you think of her? That her obsessive mobile use during team meetings is demoralizing? That people roll their eyes about her compulsive control of the smallest details of every project?

You see your boss in a variety of settings—client and team meetings, presentations, one-on-ones, negotiations—which gives you insight into her strengths and weaknesses. But even if your observations could be helpful, is it your place to share them with her? Could frank feedback put your job or your relationship at risk?

Providing feedback to your boss, commonly called **upward feedback,** is a tricky process to master. But if you offer it correctly, your insight can not only help your boss, it can also improve your relationship with her.

Adapted from content posted on hbr.org on March 24, 2010

What the Experts Say

John Baldoni, a leadership consultant and author of *Lead Your Boss: The Subtle Art of Managing Up*, says that leadership is all about perception; if leaders don't know how others experience them, their performance suffers. And the higher up in an organization a leader sits, the harder it is to get honest feedback. Your input can help your boss see himself as others see him and help him to make critical adjustments in his behavior and approach.

Of course, giving your boss feedback requires careful thought; here are some principles to keep in mind.

The Relationship Comes First

The ability to give and receive upward feedback depends on the level of trust between you and your boss. If you know that she's unreceptive to feedback, is likely to react negatively, or if you have a rocky relationship, don't say anything. But "if your boss is open-minded and you have a good relationship," Baldoni says, "you owe her the straight talk." As with any feedback, your intentions must be good, and your desire to help your boss should supersede any issues you may have with her.

Wait to Be Invited

Even if you have a great relationship, don't launch into unsolicited feedback. Some bosses will request feedback at the end of your formal review, asking, "Is there anything else I can do to support you?" Or, when you first start working together, he may share his development areas and ask you to keep an eye out for certain behaviors that he's working on. "In a perfect world, it is a manager's responsibility to make it safe to give feedback," says Baldoni.

Of course, this is not how things usually happen. If your boss doesn't directly request feedback, ask if she would like it. This might be easiest in the context of a new project or client. You can ask something such as "Would it be useful if I occasionally check in with you about how I think the project is going?" Setting it up in advance can smooth the process, but you can also give feedback in the moment. Try asking something along the lines of "Can I tell you about something I noticed in that meeting?" Emphasize that you're trying to help her so that the client, project, or company will benefit.

Share Your Perspective

Focus your feedback on what you're actually seeing or hearing, not what *you* would do as the boss. Baldoni recommends saying things such as "I noticed that you were silent when Joe disagreed with your proposal. It can be intimidating when you don't respond to criticism." By sharing your perspective, you can help your boss see how others see him. This can be invaluable to a leader who may be disconnected from people in the lower ranks.

Focusing on your perceptions also means realizing the limitations of your standpoint—you're seeing only a partial picture of your boss's performance and all the demands he's juggling. James Detert, author of the *Harvard Business Review* articles "Why Employees Are

Afraid to Speak" and "Speaking Up to Higher-Ups," says, "Subordinates by and large don't have a full appreciation of [their bosses'] reality."

Good feedback rules still apply. Your feedback should be honest, specific, and data-driven. Open with something positive and then offer constructive comments along with suggestions for improvement. Avoid accusations.

If Your Boss Bites Back

No matter how thoughtfully you've prepared and delivered your feedback, your boss may get upset or defensive. Sometimes reframing it in terms of what your boss cares most about can help, says Detert. "Point out how specific behaviors [may be] inhibiting your boss from achieving her goals."

Gauge her reaction to determine how she prefers to receive feedback and what topics are out of bounds. Perhaps she doesn't want to receive pointers on her communication style or a certain high-pressure initiative. Rather than clamming up after a negative reaction, take the opportunity to ask her about what would be useful going forward.

When in Doubt, Hold Your Tongue

If you're not sure your boss wants feedback or if the subject in question is sensitive, it's better not to speak up. Don't risk your working relationship or your job. Instead, look for opportunities to comment anonymously, such as a 360-degree feedback process. If you feel your boss's behavior is putting the company or your unit in jeopardy, follow the appropriate channels in your company—starting with

Human Resources or your employee resource manual or wiki.

Amy Gallo is a contributing editor at *Harvard Business Review*. Follow her on Twitter at @amyegallo.

Managing Multiple Bosses

by Amy Gallo

The movie *Office Space*, a comedy about work life in a typical 1990s software company, details the saga of Peter Gibbons—a man with eight different bosses. All of them, seemingly unaware of each other, pass by his desk and tell him what to do. Although the film is most certainly a satire, for some, it's not far from the truth. Many of us report to more than one boss, so learning to handle multiple managers is essential.

What the Experts Say

"As you go to a matrixed structure, you can easily have between one and seven immediate supervisors," says Robert Sutton, the author of *Good Boss, Bad Boss*. Adam Grant, coauthor of the *Harvard Business Review* article "The Hidden Advantages of Quiet Bosses," concurs. "As com-

---

Adapted from content posted on hbr.org on August 18, 2011

panies continue to flatten, organize work around specific projects, and use temporary teams to complete projects, many employees find themselves reporting to multiple bosses," he says. Although this is more likely to happen in bigger and more complex companies, it can happen in small organizations and family-owned businesses, too. Having many bosses is complicated, and, as Grant says, "If you're not careful, you can end up letting all of them down."

Here are some guidelines to make your job, and theirs, easier.

Recognize the Challenges

Although working for more than one person can present numerous challenges, there are three common ones to watch for:

1. **Overload.** With several people assigning you work, one of the greatest risks is simply having too much to do. "If you report to multiple bosses who supervise your efforts on different tasks and projects, it's all too easy for each boss to treat you as if you have no other responsibilities," says Grant.

2. **Conflicting messages.** "The more bosses you have, the more conflicting messages you get," says Sutton. Sometimes this happens out of ignorance—your bosses aren't aware of what the others are saying—or because people are pushing their own agendas. "Different bosses often have different expectations, and what

impresses one may disappoint another," says Grant.

3. **Loyalty.** "Some bosses want to know that they're your first priority. If you have more than one boss who feels this way, it's easy to get caught in the middle," says Grant. You may need to negotiate between competing demands for your loyalty.

So, how do you make it work?

Know Who Your Ultimate Boss Is

Although you may take direction from multiple managers, most of us have one person who's ultimately responsible for our careers. Ask a lot of questions about the reporting structure. Find out who completes your reviews and who contributes to them. Who makes decisions about your compensation, promotions, and so on?

Stay Connected

Reporting to more than one person can be complicated further if your bosses are in different locations. When your bosses work remotely (or when you do), you need to overcommunicate to make up for the lack of face-to-face time. Rely on technology to help you. Make your calendar viewable to those outside the office or use a web-based tool such as Google Calendar. This will allow all your bosses to know where you are, even when they can't see you. You can use the same calendar to indicate what days you're working on which projects. To simulate the drop-by-your-desk conversations, use an instant messaging application to have brief check-ins or ask quick questions. If only one of your bosses is remote, don't inadvertently cater to the boss whom you see more often, and make sure the distant manager knows you're meeting *his* needs, too.

Be Proactive About Your Workload

Let everyone know what's on your plate. Although it may not be in your job description, it will behoove you to negotiate between your bosses. "I would err on the side of taking the initiative to coordinate between them. Most bosses prefer proactive employees," says Grant. You can create a shared document that lists all of your ongoing tasks and projects, or you can communicate these items in weekly check-in meetings.

Get Your Bosses to Communicate

Most bosses appreciate your bringing them solutions, not problems, but this is complicated when you have more than one manager. Whether you need to resolve contradictory directions, reduce your workload, or sort out inconsistent demands, the best approach is to get your bosses to talk with each other, rather than trying to represent one's agenda to the other. "Start by assuming the best. Invite them to discuss the conflicts and get them out on the table," says Sutton. Bring your bosses together in the same place—in a face-to-face meeting or on a conference call—and explain what the conflict is. Enlist them in the problem solving and push for transparency. "If you ask your bosses for advice on how to handle the disagreement, they're more likely to take your perspective and see the challenges from your point of view," says Grant.

Set Boundaries

"The most important skill for staying sane while reporting to multiple bosses is the ability to set boundaries," says Grant. He points to research done by Harvard Business School professor Leslie Perlow. She found that engineers at a *Fortune* 500 company were constantly interrupted by managers and coworkers. She helped them create norms for quiet time: Three days a week, there would be no interruptions before noon so they could focus on work. If your multiple bosses frequently come to you with questions or to check in about their projects, establish protected times. As mentioned earlier, you can block out times in your calendar for work on certain projects. Before taking on a new project, remind your bosses that you'll need to assess how it fits into your overall workload. Frame this as wanting to be sure you have enough bandwidth to do a project justice rather than putting the request off.

Get Sneaky if You Have To

The aforementioned advice works best in a *healthy* organization, but yours may not reward transparency and proactive approaches. You may find that your bosses are unresponsive or unwilling to meet with you to resolve conflicts, which requires a different approach. "If you're in a fear-based environment, you have to figure out how to protect yourself. The worse the environment, the sneakier you have to get," says Sutton. Figure out which of your bosses has the most power, and prioritize her assignments. "The smart employee doesn't ask. Instead, do your own calculation of who is more powerful and who would hurt you the least," says Sutton.

Don't Take It Personally

Sutton notes that it's easy to assume that your bosses are out to get you, but usually that's not the case. They're probably just pushing their own agendas, and you're getting caught in the middle. Try not to feel persecuted. Instead, identify the conflicts and work to resolve them.

Reap the Benefits

Despite the challenges, having more than one boss can also be an advantage. For example, you're likely to get more robust feedback. If your bosses come from different parts of the organization, you'll have access to a larger and more varied network. You probably have more autonomy because you don't have one person calling all the shots. "Like a kid playing parents off each other, ask the person who you know will give you the answer you want," says Sutton. Although this may seem underhanded, it's an effective way to align your interests with those of your bosses and the company.

Case Study: A Monday Morning To-Do List

Kim Bryant had been in the accounting industry for 15 years when she started with a new firm as a staff accountant. The company had three partners, and Kim was initially hired to work for one of them. But soon she was asked to continue her work for that partner and also help out one of the others. "The most difficult thing about working for two partners was that both had projects that they felt were urgent and it put me in an uncomfortable situation," she says. Kim had to decide which project to work on first. When she asked one of her bosses for advice, he would say he wanted his project done first. Frequently, one partner assigned her something urgent when she was working on an upcoming deadline for the other. So Kim created a to-do list every Monday morning, prioritized by due date, and shared it with the two partners. "That allowed each partner to be aware of what I had been assigned to do," she says.

She also learned to watch their schedules, often with the help of their secretary. If Kim had been told that a project was urgent, she could gauge how soon she needed to do it based on when the partner was back in the office. She knew if she got it on his desk before he returned, she would be fine.

Amy Gallo is a contributing editor at *Harvard Business Review*. Follow her on Twitter at @amyegallo.

Section 2
Managing Across

Do you depend on lots of people over whom you have no authority? Do you struggle to navigate your company's political landscape? To get your cross-functional team functioning? To collaborate across time zones? To motivate colleagues to meet *your* deadlines when they're juggling countless other projects?

Managing *across*—with peers, vendors, or consultants—is complex. You don't have a say in their reviews or decide if they get promoted. So you need to use other tactics, such as setting mutually beneficial goals, establishing your credibility, polishing your powers of persuasion, and tapping into your network. The articles in this section will give you these tools.

What Makes a Leader?

A summary of the full-length HBR article by **Daniel Goleman**, *highlighting key ideas.*

THE IDEA IN BRIEF

Are you so intent on meeting deadlines or hitting financial targets that you're neglecting working relationships? Do you often interrupt colleagues? Fail to ask them what else is on their plates?

If you nodded "yes" to any of these questions, you may have zeroed in on what's getting in the way of your ability to work well with people at all levels, across silos, and with personalities that may be very different from your own. Managing across requires *emotional intelligence*: self-awareness, self-regulation, motivation, empathy, and social skill. Developing emotional intelligence will help you better understand your own—and others'—priorities, pressures, and work styles.

Reprint #R0401H

THE IDEA IN PRACTICE

The Five Components of Emotional Intelligence

Component	Definition	Hallmarks	Example
Self-Awareness	Knowing one's emotions, strengths, weaknesses, drives, values, and goals—and their impact on others	• Self-confidence • Realistic self-assessment • Self-deprecating sense of humor • Thirst for constructive criticism	A manager knows tight deadlines bring out the worst in him. So he plans his time to get work done well in advance.
Self-Regulation	Controlling or redirecting disruptive emotions and impulses	• Trustworthiness • Integrity • Comfort with ambiguity and change	When a team botches a presentation, its leader resists the urge to scream. Instead, she considers possible reasons for the failure, explains the consequences to her team, and explores solutions with them.
Motivation	Being driven to achieve for the sake of achievement	• A passion for the work itself and for new challenges • Unflagging energy to improve • Optimism in the face of failure	A portfolio manager at an investment company sees her fund tumble for three consecutive quarters. Major clients defect. Instead of blaming external circumstances, she decides to learn from the experience—and engineers a turnaround.

Empathy	Considering others' feelings, especially when making decisions	• Expertise in attracting and retaining talent • Ability to develop others • Sensitivity to cross-cultural differences	An American consultant and her team pitch a project to a potential client in Japan. Her team interprets the client's silence as disapproval and prepares to leave. The consultant reads the client's body language and senses interest. She continues the meeting, and her team gets the job.
Social Skill	Managing relationships to move people in desired directions	• Effectiveness in leading change • Persuasiveness • Extensive networking • Expertise in building and leading teams	A manager wants his company to adopt a better Internet strategy. He finds kindred spirits and assembles a de facto team to create a prototype website. He persuades allies in other divisions to fund the company's participation in a relevant convention. His company forms an Internet division—and puts him in charge of it.

It was Daniel Goleman who first brought the term "emotional intelligence" to a wide audience with his 1995 book of that name, and it was Goleman who first applied the concept to business with his 1998 HBR article, reprinted here. In his research at nearly 200 large, global companies, Goleman found that while the qualities traditionally associated with leadership— such as intelligence, toughness, determination, and vision—are required for success, they are insufficient. Truly effective leaders are also distinguished by a high degree of emotional intelligence, which includes self-awareness, self-regulation, motivation, empathy, and social skill.

These qualities may sound "soft" and unbusiness-like, but Goleman found direct ties between emotional intelligence and measurable business results. While emotional intelligence's relevance to business has continued to spark debate over the past six years, Goleman's article remains the definitive reference on the subject, with a description of each component of emotional intelligence and a detailed discussion of how to recognize it in potential leaders, how and why it connects to performance, and how it can be learned.

Every businessperson knows a story about a highly intelligent, highly skilled executive who was promoted into a leadership position only to fail at the job. And they also know a story about someone with solid—but not extraordinary—intellectual abilities and technical skills who was promoted into a similar position and then soared.

Such anecdotes support the widespread belief that identifying individuals with the "right stuff" to be leaders is more art than science. After all, the personal styles of superb leaders vary: Some leaders are subdued and analytical; others shout their manifestos from the mountaintops. And just as important, different situations call for different types of leadership. Most mergers need a sensitive negotiator at the helm, whereas many turnarounds require a more forceful authority.

I have found, however, that the most effective leaders are alike in one crucial way: They all have a high degree of what has come to be known as *emotional intelligence.* It's not that IQ and technical skills are irrelevant. They do matter, but mainly as "threshold capabilities"; that is, they are the entry-level requirements for executive positions. But my research, along with other recent studies, clearly shows that emotional intelligence is the sine qua non of leadership. Without it, a person can have the best training in the world, an incisive, analytical mind, and an endless supply of smart ideas, but he still won't make a great leader.

In the course of the past year, my colleagues and I have focused on how emotional intelligence operates at work. We have examined the relationship between emotional intelligence and effective performance, especially in leaders. And we have observed how emotional intelligence shows itself on the job. How can you tell if someone has high emotional intelligence, for example, and how can you recognize it in yourself? In the following pages, we'll explore these questions, taking each of the components of emotional intelligence—self-awareness, self-regulation, motivation, empathy, and social skill— in turn.

Evaluating Emotional Intelligence

Most large companies today have employed trained psychologists to develop what are known as "competency models" to aid them in identifying, training, and promoting likely stars in the leadership firmament. The psychologists have also developed such models for lower-level positions. And in recent years, I have analyzed competency models from 188 companies, most of which were large and global and included the likes of Lucent Technologies, British Airways, and Credit Suisse.

In carrying out this work, my objective was to determine which personal capabilities drove outstanding performance within these organizations, and to what degree they did so. I grouped capabilities into three categories: purely technical skills like accounting and business planning; cognitive abilities like analytical reasoning; and competencies demonstrating emotional intelligence, such as the ability to work with others and effectiveness in leading change.

To create some of the competency models, psychologists asked senior managers at the companies to identify the capabilities that typified the organization's most outstanding leaders. To create other models, the psychologists used objective criteria, such as a division's profitability, to differentiate the star performers at senior levels within their organizations from the average ones. Those individuals were then extensively interviewed and tested, and their capabilities were compared. This process resulted in the creation of lists of ingredients for highly effective leaders. The lists ranged in length from seven to 15 items and included such ingredients as initiative and strategic vision.

When I analyzed all this data, I found dramatic results. To be sure, intellect was a driver of outstanding performance. Cognitive skills such as big-picture thinking and long-term vision were particularly important. But when I calculated the ratio of technical skills, IQ, and emotional intelligence as ingredients of excellent performance, emotional intelligence proved to be twice as important as the others for jobs at all levels.

Moreover, my analysis showed that emotional intelligence played an increasingly important role at the highest levels of the company, where differences in technical skills are of negligible importance. In other words, the higher the rank of a person considered to be a star performer, the more emotional intelligence capabilities showed up as the reason for his or her effectiveness. When I compared star performers with average ones in senior leadership positions, nearly 90% of the difference in their profiles was attributable to emotional intelligence factors rather than cognitive abilities.

Other researchers have confirmed that emotional intelligence not only distinguishes outstanding leaders but can also be linked to strong performance. The findings of the late David McClelland, the renowned researcher in human and organizational behavior, are a good example. In a 1996 study of a global food and beverage company, McClelland found that when senior managers had a critical mass of emotional intelligence capabilities, their divisions outperformed yearly earnings goals by 20%. Meanwhile, division leaders without that critical mass underperformed by almost the same amount. McClelland's findings, interestingly, held as true in the company's U.S. divisions as in its divisions in Asia and Europe.

In short, the numbers are beginning to tell us a persuasive story about the link between a company's success and the emotional intelligence of its leaders. And just as important, research is also demonstrating that people can, if they take the right approach, develop their emotional intelligence. (See the sidebar "Can Emotional Intelligence Be Learned?")

Self-Awareness

Self-awareness is the first component of emotional intelligence—which makes sense when one considers that the Delphic oracle gave the advice to "know thyself" thousands of years ago. Self-awareness means having a deep understanding of one's emotions, strengths, weaknesses, needs, and drives. People with strong self-awareness are neither overly critical nor unrealistically hopeful. Rather, they are honest—with themselves and with others.

People who have a high degree of self-awareness recognize how their feelings affect them, other people, and their job performance. Thus, a self-aware person who knows that tight deadlines bring out the worst in him plans his time carefully and gets his work done well in advance. Another person with high self-awareness will

The Five Components of Emotional Intelligence at Work

	Definition	Hallmarks
Self-Awareness	the ability to recognize and understand your moods, emotions, and drives, as well as their effect on others	self-confidence realistic self-assessment self-deprecating sense of humor
Self-Regulation	the ability to control or redirect disruptive impulses and moods the propensity to suspend judgment—to think before acting	trustworthiness and integrity comfort with ambiguity openness to change
Motivation	a passion to work for reasons that go beyond money or status a propensity to pursue goals with energy and persistence	strong drive to achieve optimism, even in the face of failure organizational commitment
Empathy	the ability to understand the emotional makeup of other people skill in treating people according to their emotional reactions	expertise in building and retaining talent cross-cultural sensitivity service to clients and customers
Social Skill	proficiency in managing relationships and building networks an ability to find common ground and build rapport	effectiveness in leading change persuasiveness expertise in building and leading teams

be able to work with a demanding client. She will understand the client's impact on her moods and the deeper reasons for her frustration. "Their trivial demands take us away from the real work that needs to be done," she might explain. And she will go one step further and turn her anger into something constructive.

CAN EMOTIONAL INTELLIGENCE BE LEARNED?

For ages, people have debated if leaders are born or made. So too goes the debate about emotional intelligence. Are people born with certain levels of empathy, for example, or do they acquire empathy as a result of life's experiences? The answer is both. Scientific inquiry strongly suggests that there is a genetic component to emotional intelligence. Psychological and developmental research indicates that nurture plays a role as well. How much of each perhaps will never be known, but research and practice clearly demonstrate that emotional intelligence can be learned.

One thing is certain: Emotional intelligence increases with age. There is an old-fashioned word for the phenomenon: maturity. Yet even with maturity, some people still need training to enhance their emotional intelligence. Unfortunately, far too many training programs that intend to build leadership skills—including emotional intelligence—are a waste of time and money. The problem is simple: They focus on the wrong part of the brain.

Emotional intelligence is born largely in the neurotransmitters of the brain's limbic system, which governs feelings, impulses, and drives. Research indicates that the limbic system learns best through motivation, extended practice, and feedback. Compare this with the kind of learning that goes on in the neocortex, which governs analytical and technical ability.

The neocortex grasps concepts and logic. It is the part of the brain that figures out how to use a computer or make a sales call by reading a book. Not surprisingly—but mistakenly—it is also the part of the brain targeted by most training programs aimed at enhancing emotional intelligence. When such programs take, in effect, a neocortical approach, my research with the Consortium for Research on Emotional Intelligence in Organizations has shown they can even have a *negative* impact on people's job performance.

To enhance emotional intelligence, organizations must refocus their training to include the limbic system. They must help people break old behavioral habits and establish new ones. That not only takes much more time than conventional training programs, it also requires an individualized approach.

Imagine an executive who is thought to be low on empathy by her colleagues. Part of that deficit shows itself as an inability to listen; she interrupts people and doesn't pay close attention to what they're saying. To fix the problem, the executive needs to be motivated to change, and then she needs practice and feedback from others in the company. A colleague or coach could be tapped to let the executive know when she has been observed failing to listen. She would then have to replay the incident and give a better response;

(continued)

(*continued*)

that is, demonstrate her ability to absorb what others are saying. And the executive could be directed to observe certain executives who listen well and to mimic their behavior.

With persistence and practice, such a process can lead to lasting results. I know one Wall Street executive who sought to improve his empathy—specifically his ability to read people's reactions and see their perspectives. Before beginning his quest, the executive's subordinates were terrified of working with him. People even went so far as to hide bad news from him. Naturally, he was shocked when finally confronted with these facts. He went home and told his family—but they only confirmed what he had heard at work. When their opinions on any given subject did not mesh with his, they, too, were frightened of him.

Enlisting the help of a coach, the executive went to work to heighten his empathy through practice and feedback. His first step was to take a vacation to a foreign country where he did not speak the language. While there, he monitored his reactions to the unfamiliar and his openness to people who were different from him. When he returned home, humbled by his week abroad, the executive asked his coach to shadow him for parts of the day, several times a week, to critique how he treated people with new or different perspectives. At the same time, he consciously used on-the-job interactions as opportunities to practice "hearing" ideas that differed from his. Finally, the executive had himself videotaped in meetings and asked those who worked for and with him to critique his ability to acknowledge and understand the feelings of others. It took several months, but the executive's emotional intelligence did ultimately rise, and the improvement was reflected in his overall performance on the job.

It's important to emphasize that building one's emotional intelligence cannot—will not—happen without sincere desire and concerted effort. A brief seminar won't help; nor can one buy a how-to manual. It is much harder to learn to empathize—to internalize empathy as a natural response to people—than it is to become adept at regression analysis. But it can be done. "Nothing great was ever achieved without enthusiasm," wrote Ralph Waldo Emerson. If your goal is to become a real leader, these words can serve as a guidepost in your efforts to develop high emotional intelligence.

Self-awareness extends to a person's understanding of his or her values and goals. Someone who is highly self-aware knows where he is headed and why; so, for example, he will be able to be firm in turning down a job offer that is tempting financially but does not fit with his principles or long-term goals. A person who lacks self-awareness is apt to make decisions that bring on inner turmoil by treading on buried values. "The money looked good so I signed on," someone might say two years into a job, "but the work means so little to me that I'm constantly bored." The decisions of self-aware people mesh with their values; consequently, they often find work to be energizing.

How can one recognize self-awareness? First and foremost, it shows itself as candor and an ability to assess oneself realistically. People with high self-awareness are able to speak accurately and openly—although not necessarily effusively or confessionally—about their emotions and the impact they have on their work. For instance, one manager I know of was skeptical about a new personal-shopper service that her company, a major department-store chain, was about to introduce. Without prompting from her team or her boss, she offered them an explanation: "It's hard for me to get behind the rollout of this service," she admitted, "because I really wanted to run the project, but I wasn't selected. Bear with me while I deal with that." The manager did indeed examine her feelings; a week later, she was supporting the project fully.

Such self-knowledge often shows itself in the hiring process. Ask a candidate to describe a time he got carried away by his feelings and did something he later regretted. Self-aware candidates will be frank in admitting to failure—and will often tell their tales with a smile. One of the hallmarks of self-awareness is a self-deprecating sense of humor.

Self-awareness can also be identified during performance reviews. Self-aware people know—and are comfortable talking about—their limitations and strengths, and they often demonstrate a thirst for constructive criticism. By contrast, people with low self-awareness interpret the message that they need to improve as a threat or a sign of failure.

Self-aware people can also be recognized by their self-confidence. They have a firm grasp of their capabilities and are less likely to set themselves up to fail by, for example, overstretching on assignments. They know, too, when to ask for help. And the risks they take on the job are calculated. They won't ask for a challenge that they know they can't handle alone. They'll play to their strengths.

Consider the actions of a midlevel employee who was invited to sit in on a strategy meeting with her company's top executives. Although she was the most junior person in the room, she did not sit there quietly, listening in awestruck or fearful silence. She knew she had a head for clear logic and the skill to present ideas persuasively, and she offered cogent suggestions about the company's strategy. At the same time, her self-awareness stopped her from wandering into territory where she knew she was weak.

Despite the value of having self-aware people in the workplace, my research indicates that senior executives don't often give self-awareness the credit it deserves when they look for potential leaders. Many executives mistake candor about feelings for "wimpiness" and fail to give due respect to employees who openly acknowledge their shortcomings. Such people are too readily dismissed as "not tough enough" to lead others.

In fact, the opposite is true. In the first place, people generally admire and respect candor. Furthermore, leaders are constantly required to make judgment calls that require a candid assessment of capabilities—their own and those of others. Do we have the management expertise to acquire a competitor? Can we launch a new product within six months? People who assess themselves honestly—that is, self-aware people—are well suited to do the same for the organizations they run.

Self-Regulation

Biological impulses drive our emotions. We cannot do away with them—but we can do much to manage them. Self-regulation, which is like an ongoing inner conversation, is the component of emotional intelligence that frees us from being prisoners of our feelings. People engaged in such a conversation feel bad moods and emotional impulses just as everyone else does, but they find ways to control them and even to channel them in useful ways.

Imagine an executive who has just watched a team of his employees present a botched analysis to the company's board of directors. In the gloom that follows, the executive might find himself tempted to pound on the table in anger or kick over a chair. He could leap up and scream at the group. Or he might maintain a grim silence, glaring at everyone before stalking off.

But if he had a gift for self-regulation, he would choose a different approach. He would pick his words carefully, acknowledging the team's poor performance without rushing to any hasty judgment. He would then step back to consider the reasons for the failure. Are they personal—a lack of effort? Are there any mitigating factors? What was his role in the debacle? After considering these questions, he would call the team together, lay out the incident's consequences, and offer his feelings about it. He would then present his analysis of the problem and a well-considered solution.

Why does self-regulation matter so much for leaders? First of all, people who are in control of their feelings and impulses—that is, people who are reasonable—are able to create an environment of trust and fairness. In such an environment, politics and infighting are sharply reduced and productivity is high. Talented people flock to the organization and aren't tempted to leave. And self-regulation has a trickle-down effect. No one wants to be known as a hothead when the boss is known for her calm approach. Fewer bad moods at the top mean fewer throughout the organization.

Second, self-regulation is important for competitive reasons. Everyone knows that business today is rife with ambiguity and change. Companies merge and break apart regularly. Technology transforms work at a dizzying pace. People who have mastered their emotions are able to roll with the changes. When a new program is announced, they don't panic; instead, they are able to suspend judgment, seek out information, and listen to the executives as they explain the new program. As the initiative moves forward, these people are able to move with it.

Sometimes they even lead the way. Consider the case of a manager at a large manufacturing company. Like her colleagues, she had used a certain software program for five years. The program drove how she collected and reported data and how she thought about the company's strategy. One day, senior executives announced that a new program was to be installed that would radically change how information was gathered and assessed within the organization. While many people in the company complained bitterly about how disruptive the change would be, the manager mulled over the reasons for the new program and was convinced of its potential to improve performance. She eagerly attended training sessions—some of her colleagues refused to do so—and was eventually promoted to run several divisions, in part because she used the new technology so effectively.

I want to push the importance of self-regulation to leadership even further and make the case that it enhances integrity, which is not only a personal virtue but also an organizational strength. Many of the bad things that happen in companies are a function of impulsive behavior. People rarely plan to exaggerate profits, pad expense accounts, dip into the till, or abuse power for selfish ends. Instead, an opportunity presents itself, and people with low impulse control just say yes.

By contrast, consider the behavior of the senior executive at a large food company. The executive was scrupulously honest in his negotiations with local distributors. He would routinely lay out his cost structure in detail, thereby giving the distributors a realistic understanding of the company's pricing. This approach meant the executive couldn't always drive a hard bargain. Now, on occasion, he felt the urge to increase profits by withholding information about the company's costs. But he challenged that impulse—he saw that it made more sense in the long run to counteract it. His emotional self-regulation paid off in strong, lasting relationships with distributors that benefited the company more than any short-term financial gains would have.

The signs of emotional self-regulation, therefore, are easy to see: a propensity for reflection and thoughtfulness; comfort with ambiguity and change; and integrity—an ability to say no to impulsive urges.

Like self-awareness, self-regulation often does not get its due. People who can master their emotions are sometimes seen as cold fish—their considered responses are taken as a lack of passion. People with fiery temperaments are frequently thought of as "classic" leaders—their outbursts are considered hallmarks of charisma and power. But when such people make it to the top, their impulsiveness often works against them. In my research, extreme displays of negative emotion have never emerged as a driver of good leadership.

Motivation

If there is one trait that virtually all effective leaders have, it is motivation. They are driven to achieve beyond expectations—their own and everyone else's. The key word here is *achieve*. Plenty of people are motivated by external factors, such as a big salary or the status that comes from having an impressive title or being part of a prestigious company. By contrast, those with leadership potential are motivated by a deeply embedded desire to achieve for the sake of achievement.

If you are looking for leaders, how can you identify people who are motivated by the drive to achieve rather than by external rewards? The first sign is a passion for the work itself—such people seek out creative challenges, love to learn, and take great pride in a job well done. They also display an unflagging energy to do things better. People with such energy often seem restless with the status quo. They are persistent with their questions about why things are done one way rather than another; they are eager to explore new approaches to their work.

A cosmetics company manager, for example, was frustrated that he had to wait two weeks to get sales results from people in the field. He finally tracked down an automated phone system that would beep each of his salespeople at 5 p.m. every day. An automated message then prompted them to punch in their numbers—how many calls and sales they had made that day. The system shortened the feedback time on sales results from weeks to hours.

That story illustrates two other common traits of people who are driven to achieve. They are forever raising the performance bar, and they like to keep score. Take the performance bar first. During performance reviews, people with high levels of motivation might ask to be "stretched" by their superiors. Of course, an employee who combines self-awareness with internal motivation will recognize her limits—but she won't settle for objectives that seem too easy to fulfill.

And it follows naturally that people who are driven to do better also want a way of tracking progress—their own, their team's, and their company's. Whereas people with low achievement motivation are often fuzzy about results, those with high achievement motivation often keep score by tracking such hard measures as profitability or market share. I know of a money manager who starts and ends his day on the Internet, gauging the performance of his stock fund against four industry-set benchmarks.

Interestingly, people with high motivation remain optimistic even when the score is against them. In such cases, self-regulation combines with achievement motivation to overcome the frustration and depression that come after a setback or failure. Take the case of an another portfolio manager at a large investment company. After several successful years, her fund tumbled for three consecutive quarters, leading three large institutional clients to shift their business elsewhere.

Some executives would have blamed the nosedive on circumstances outside their control; others might have seen the setback as evidence of personal failure. This portfolio manager, however, saw an opportunity to prove she could lead a turnaround. Two years later, when she was promoted to a very senior level in the company, she described the experience as "the best thing that ever happened to me; I learned so much from it."

Executives trying to recognize high levels of achievement motivation in their people can look for one last piece of evidence: commitment to the organization. When people love their jobs for the work itself, they often feel committed to the organizations that make that work possible. Committed employees are likely to stay with an organization even when they are pursued by headhunters waving money.

It's not difficult to understand how and why a motivation to achieve translates into strong leadership. If you set the performance bar high for yourself, you will do the same for the organization when you are in a position to do so. Likewise, a drive to surpass goals and an interest in keeping score can be contagious. Leaders with these traits can often build a team of managers around them with the same traits. And of course, optimism and organizational commitment are fundamental to leadership— just try to imagine running a company without them.

Empathy

Of all the dimensions of emotional intelligence, empathy is the most easily recognized. We have all felt the empathy of a sensitive teacher or friend; we have all been struck by its absence in an unfeeling coach or boss. But when it comes to business, we rarely hear people praised, let alone rewarded, for their empathy. The very word seems unbusinesslike, out of place amid the tough realities of the marketplace.

But empathy doesn't mean a kind of "I'm OK, you're OK" mushiness. For a leader, that is, it doesn't mean adopting other people's emotions as one's own and trying to please everybody. That would be a nightmare—it would make action impossible. Rather, empathy means thoughtfully considering employees' feelings—along with other factors—in the process of making intelligent decisions.

For an example of empathy in action, consider what happened when two giant brokerage companies merged, creating redundant jobs in all their divisions. One division manager called his people together and gave a gloomy speech that emphasized the number of people who would soon be fired. The manager of another division gave his people a different kind of speech. He was up-front about his own worry and confusion, and he promised to keep people informed and to treat everyone fairly.

The difference between these two managers was empathy. The first manager was too worried about his own fate to consider the feelings of his anxiety-stricken colleagues. The second knew intuitively what his people were feeling, and he acknowledged their fears with his words. Is it any surprise that the first manager saw his division sink as many demoralized people, especially the most talented, departed? By contrast, the second manager continued to be a strong leader, his best people stayed, and his division remained as productive as ever.

Empathy is particularly important today as a component of leadership for at least three reasons: the increasing use of teams; the rapid pace of globalization; and the growing need to retain talent.

Consider the challenge of leading a team. As anyone who has ever been a part of one can attest, teams are cauldrons of bubbling emotions. They are often charged with reaching a consensus—which is hard enough with two people and much more difficult as the numbers increase. Even in groups with as few as four or five members, alliances form and clashing agendas get set. A team's leader must be able to sense and understand the viewpoints of everyone around the table.

That's exactly what a marketing manager at a large information technology company was able to do when she was appointed to lead a troubled team. The group was in turmoil, overloaded by work and missing deadlines. Tensions were high among the members. Tinkering with procedures was not enough to bring the group together and make it an effective part of the company.

So the manager took several steps. In a series of one-on-one sessions, she took the time to listen to everyone in the group—what was frustrating them, how they rated their colleagues, whether they felt they had been ignored. And then she directed the team in a way that brought it together: She encouraged people to speak more openly about their frustrations, and she helped people raise constructive complaints during meetings. In short, her empathy allowed her to understand her team's emotional makeup. The result was not just heightened collaboration among members but also added business, as the team was called on for help by a wider range of internal clients.

Globalization is another reason for the rising importance of empathy for business leaders. Cross-cultural dialogue can easily lead to miscues and misunderstandings. Empathy is an antidote. People who have it are attuned to subtleties in body language; they can hear the message beneath the words being spoken. Beyond that, they have a deep understanding of both the existence and the importance of cultural and ethnic differences.

Consider the case of an American consultant whose team had just pitched a project to a potential Japanese client. In its dealings with Americans, the team was accustomed to being bombarded with questions after such a proposal, but this time it was greeted with a long silence. Other members of the team, taking the silence as disapproval, were ready to pack and leave. The lead consultant gestured them to stop. Although he was not particularly familiar with Japanese culture, he read the client's face and posture and sensed not rejection but interest—even deep consideration. He was right: When the client finally spoke, it was to give the consulting firm the job.

Finally, empathy plays a key role in the retention of talent, particularly in today's information economy. Leaders have always needed empathy to develop and keep good people, but today the stakes are higher. When good people leave, they take the company's knowledge with them.

That's where coaching and mentoring come in. It has repeatedly been shown that coaching and mentoring pay off not just in better performance but also in increased job satisfaction and decreased turnover. But what makes coaching and mentoring work best is the nature of the relationship. Outstanding coaches and mentors get inside the heads of the people they are helping. They sense how to give effective feedback. They know when to push for better performance and when to hold back. In the way they motivate their protégés, they demonstrate empathy in action.

In what is probably sounding like a refrain, let me repeat that empathy doesn't get much respect in business. People wonder how leaders can make hard decisions if they are "feeling" for all the people who will be affected. But leaders with empathy do more than sympathize with people around them: They use their knowledge to improve their companies in subtle but important ways.

Social Skill

The first three components of emotional intelligence are self-management skills. The last two, empathy and social skill, concern a person's ability to manage relationships with others. As a component of emotional intelligence, social skill is not as simple as it sounds. It's not just a matter of friendliness, although people with high levels of social skill are rarely mean-spirited. Social skill, rather, is friendliness with a purpose: moving people in the direction you desire, whether that's agreement on a new marketing strategy or enthusiasm about a new product.

Socially skilled people tend to have a wide circle of acquaintances, and they have a knack for finding common ground with people of all kinds—a knack for building rapport. That doesn't mean they socialize continually; it means they work according to the assumption that nothing important gets done alone. Such people have a network in place when the time for action comes.

Social skill is the culmination of the other dimensions of emotional intelligence. People tend to be very effective at managing relationships when they can understand and control their own emotions and can empathize with the feelings of others. Even motivation contributes to social skill. Remember that people who are driven to achieve tend to be optimistic, even in the face of setbacks or failure. When people are upbeat, their "glow" is cast upon conversations and other social encounters. They are popular, and for good reason.

Because it is the outcome of the other dimensions of emotional intelligence, social skill is recognizable on the job in many ways that will by now sound familiar. Socially skilled people, for instance, are adept at managing teams—that's their empathy at work. Likewise, they are expert persuaders—a manifestation of self-awareness, self-regulation, and empathy combined. Given those skills, good persuaders know when to make an emotional plea, for instance, and when an appeal to reason will work better. And motivation, when publicly visible, makes such people excellent collaborators; their passion for the work spreads to others, and they are driven to find solutions.

But sometimes social skill shows itself in ways the other emotional intelligence components do not. For instance, socially skilled people may at times appear not to be working while at work. They seem to be idly schmoozing—chatting in the hallways with colleagues or joking around with people who are not even connected to their "real" jobs. Socially skilled people, however, don't think it makes sense to arbitrarily limit the scope of their relationships. They build bonds widely because they know that in these fluid times, they may need help someday from people they are just getting to know today.

For example, consider the case of an executive in the strategy department of a global computer manufacturer.

By 1993, he was convinced that the company's future lay with the Internet. Over the course of the next year, he found kindred spirits and used his social skill to stitch together a virtual community that cut across levels, divisions, and nations. He then used this de facto team to put up a corporate website, among the first by a major company. And, on his own initiative, with no budget or formal status, he signed up the company to participate in an annual Internet industry convention. Calling on his allies and persuading various divisions to donate funds, he recruited more than 50 people from a dozen different units to represent the company at the convention.

Management took notice: Within a year of the conference, the executive's team formed the basis for the company's first Internet division, and he was formally put in charge of it. To get there, the executive had ignored conventional boundaries, forging and maintaining connections with people in every corner of the organization.

Is social skill considered a key leadership capability in most companies? The answer is yes, especially when compared with the other components of emotional intelligence. People seem to know intuitively that leaders need to manage relationships effectively; no leader is an island. After all, the leader's task is to get work done through other people, and social skill makes that possible. A leader who cannot express her empathy may as well not have it at all. And a leader's motivation will be useless if he cannot communicate his passion to the organization. Social skill allows leaders to put their emotional intelligence to work.

It would be foolish to assert that good-old-fashioned IQ and technical ability are not important ingredients in strong leadership. But the recipe would not be complete without emotional intelligence. It was once thought that the components of emotional intelligence were "nice to have" in business leaders. But now we know that, for the sake of performance, these are ingredients that leaders "need to have."

It is fortunate, then, that emotional intelligence can be learned. The process is not easy. It takes time and, most of all, commitment. But the benefits that come from having a well-developed emotional intelligence, both for the individual and for the organization, make it worth the effort.

———————

Daniel Goleman is the author of *Emotional Intelligence* (Bantam, 1995) and a coauthor of *Primal Leadership: Realizing the Power of Emotional Intelligence* (Harvard Business School, 2002). He is the cochairman of the Consortium for Research on Emotional Intelligence in Organizations, which is based at Rutgers University's Graduate School of Applied and Professional Psychology in Piscataway, New Jersey. He can be reached at Daniel. Goleman@verizon.net.

The Discipline of Teams

A summary of the full-length HBR article by **Jon R. Katzenbach** *and* **Douglas K. Smith,** *highlighting key ideas.*

THE IDEA IN BRIEF

Managing across is especially challenging when you're leading a group of colleagues. You're not their boss, but on this project, you're their leader. How can you get them to focus on *your* team's work when they also need to tend their own small fires—or meet *their* bosses' demands?

When you instill in your group the **discipline of teams,** your struggles will diminish. You'll be helping your team create a shared vision and then realize that vision with individual and mutual accountability.

Reprint #R0507P

THE IDEA IN PRACTICE

A team's essential discipline includes these characteristics:

1. **A meaningful common purpose the team helps shape.** Most teams are responding to an initial corporate mandate. But to be successful, your team must "own" this purpose by developing its own spin on it. For example, if one of your company's strategic priorities is to increase customer retention, how might your web team translate that into its common purpose? By committing itself to becoming the online destination of choice for B2C customers in your industry.

2. **Specific performance goals that flow from the common purpose.** Developing compelling and measurable goals will inspire and challenge your team, and inject a sense of urgency. Shared goals also have a leveling effect. They require everyone to focus on their collective effort rather than on any differences in their titles or status.

   For example, your web team might set the following goals on its way to becoming the online destination of choice for its B2C customers: 1) Increase first-time visitors to the site by 50% over last year; 2) grow repeat site visitors by 25% over last year; 3) boost e-commerce sales by 15% over last year.

3. **A strong commitment to how the work gets done.** Your team must agree on who will do what jobs, how you will establish and honor schedules, and how you will make and modify decisions. On a genuine team, everyone does equivalent amounts of real work; all members—even you as leader—contribute in concrete ways to the team's collective work.

   Developing these rules of conduct at the outset will help your team achieve its purpose and goals. The most critical rules pertain to attendance (for example, "if you can't make a meeting, send notes or a representative who can speak for you"); focus ("no checking e-mail during meetings"); discussion ("no sacred cows"); confidentiality ("the only things to leave this room are what we agree on"); analytic approach ("base decisions on data, not assumptions"); end-product orientation ("everyone gets assignments and does them"); constructive confrontation ("no finger pointing"); and, often the most important, contributions ("everyone does real work").

4. **Mutual accountability.** You can't force trust and commitment. The process of creating and agreeing upon purpose and goals helps your team members forge their accountability to one another—not just to you, the leader.

   For example, as your web team makes progress toward its three goals, everyone becomes increasingly eager to contribute to the team's success. Individuals volunteer their own and others' areas of expertise: The person with the best eye for visual detail prepares the Power-Point presentation for the next unit meeting; the one who has the strongest relationship with your IT director spearheads delicate conversations about prioritizing the team's technology needs.

Jon R. Katzenbach is a founder and senior partner of Katzenbach Partners, a strategic and organizational consulting firm, and a former director of McKinsey & Company. His most recent book is *Why Pride Matters More Than Money: The Power of the World's Greatest Motivational Force* (Crown Business, 2003). **Douglas K. Smith** is an organizational consultant and a former partner at McKinsey & Company. His most recent book is *On Value and Values: Thinking Differently About We in an Age of Me* (Financial Times Prentice Hall, 2004).

Managing Remote Relationships

by Karen Dillon

After you've dialed someone into a meeting, do you find it difficult to meaningfully involve her in the conversation—and make her *feel* involved? I've been there hundreds of times. I've even caught myself rolling my eyes as the person on the other end of that star-shaped phone breathed too loudly, spoke at the wrong time, or worst of all, didn't stop talking when everyone else was willing her to do so.

But then I began working on overseas assignments, and it was *my* voice in the dreaded "box"—so I started to see things differently. It's horrible trying to call in when people are chitchatting and making noises with their chairs. And you can never quite read the unspoken tone of the meeting. You talk too much because you want people to know you're there and at full attention. Or you talk too little because you can't figure out when it's appropriate to break in.

Though many of us work with remote colleagues and partners—or work remotely ourselves—we struggle to manage relationships with people we don't run into at the coffee station every day. That doesn't have to be the case. You *can* build strong connections. Here's what's worked in my experience.

If You're Working with Someone Remote . . .

Talk openly about the challenges

Whether you're managing a remote employee, working peer-to-peer, or partnering with someone at another company, it helps to frankly discuss the challenges as you both see them. Clarify expectations up front, and the remote worker will become more productive—and happier. When I managed a West Coast employee from an East Coast office, for example, she initially thought I expected her to immediately jump on phone calls and e-mail queries. What I actually wanted was for her to be a vibrant contributor of ideas and work; to be aware of what her East Coast colleagues were working on, helping them when possible; and to have a clear sense of how she fit into the organization. Until we directly discussed that, she slavishly sat at her desk while I imagined she was out mining her area for ideas and people. We swiftly resolved this misunderstanding with a single conversation.

Without peers in the next cubicle to informally guide them, remote employees will make basic mistakes early on, despite their good intentions, so it's also crucial to be candid with them. Perhaps they've excessively charged expenses to a corporate account, for example, or spent too much time on a low-priority project. Let them know right away. Of course, it's best practice to offer timely feedback to *all* employees, but it's especially important for remote workers. Help them correct course before a few innocent, early errors become a troublesome pattern of behavior.

Err on the side of overcommunicating

Set up regular times to catch up on the phone. As an on-site manager, I decided every two weeks felt about right for formal check-ins with my remote colleagues, with the proviso that we could talk whenever an issue arose. I was always grateful to people who came to those conversations with an agenda and a list of questions or comments (ideally sent in advance). That meant I didn't have the burden of guessing what their needs might be. It was, however, my responsibility to keep them up to date and give them information that would help them work effectively with people on-site (for example, "Joe's in meetings all day— best time to catch him is first thing in the morning"). Otherwise, they wouldn't know the right questions to ask.

Keep a running list of things to share with your remote colleagues or partners; don't assume they're copied on important announcements about your company or division. When I began working off-site, I was surprised at how much I couldn't pick up simply by keeping up with e-mail. People were hired. Projects were canceled. Desirable assignments were handed out. And I missed it all.

Sometimes even little details are critical to share— the fact that someone has had a death in the family, for example, or is under the gun for a big project deadline and won't likely be responsive this week unless it's critical. Communicate decisions large and small. E-mail, scheduled phone calls—figure out what works for your situation, and make a commitment to follow whatever protocol you mutually agree is best.

Remember time zones

It's simple, but easy to forget. Suppose you're based at your company's headquarters in New York and you have a remote colleague in Paris. You might not dive into your day until 9 a.m. your time—and that's 3 p.m. for the guy in France. So you've got about two hours of reliable overlap. If multiple people in New York want time from him, those two hours will be packed. You're sharing that window with others, so be thoughtful about what you're asking for during that time.

And respect your remote colleagues' after-hours time. When I was working in Paris for a company with a New York headquarters, I regularly fielded calls at 11 at night—5 p.m. EST. People forgot to call me until it became urgent at the end of *their* day to finish something. Set up reminders in your calendar to get in touch with remote colleagues while they're still on the clock, and don't ask them to join late calls if you can easily brief them the next day. Be clear about which meetings they can skip. They'll be much happier to take an occasional urgent call at 11 p.m. if most of your business is conducted at times that suit you both.

When you can, take *advantage* of time differences. As a manager, I loved assigning work to someone in an earlier time zone because when I came in the next morning, it would be in my inbox, ready for my attention.

Use technology to collaborate

Technology makes it easy to work with remote colleagues or partners. All it takes is a laptop to videoconference— you can bring it into any room and include someone in a meeting. With Google Docs, you and colleagues located elsewhere can simultaneously work on a file and watch one another's color-coded edits or comments appear in real time. Dropbox allows you to work on documents and then post them in a secure, cloud-based system others can easily access through the Internet.

Some companies, like Nokia, rely on instant messaging to keep remote (and local) employees in the loop. Others, like Royal Dutch Shell, host online events to get colleagues comfortable collaborating across time zones and geographical boundaries. (Shell conducted a three-day "jam" that brought together 8,200 employees from 117 countries to develop new ways to use technology to work with each other.) There's no need for someone in a satellite office to *feel* remote if you take advantage of the tools that are readily available to companies of all sizes.

If You're the Remote Colleague . . .

Make sure you're up to the challenge—
and take responsibility

To integrate with a team that's located somewhere else, you have to be fearless about picking up the phone, asking to be briefed, and telling people when conference calls won't work in your time zone. You have to keep on top of a schedule when no one is around to remind you of important meetings or events. Self-starters required.

Make it clear to people that you're *present*, intellectually and physically, and dedicated to packing a lot into your day. When you speak up in a conversation, participate in a brainstorming session, or respond to an e-mail query, make sure it's a thoughtful contribution—not just a token gesture to prove that you're paying attention. Think about your colleagues and their projects and challenges, even when you're not being asked to do so. One of the most successful remote employees I've ever managed would periodically come back from an inspiring business lunch with a great connection for another colleague or send a link to a thought-provoking article that might aid a peer. She felt like a part of a team that way, not just someone covering a different territory.

Even after you've established positive relationships and earned your colleagues' trust, recognize that the burden is often on you, the remote employee, to make things work. Show your colleagues what you bring to the table. Volunteer to help with projects when you have relevant ideas or expertise. Follow social media buzz on your company or industry—and then share updates with colleagues. If you always think of yourself as part of a team, not a soloist, you'll naturally consider how your work can help others.

Partner with the home office

Work closely with the home office to establish expectations. Should you match your colleagues' hours? Is it OK to be out for appointments without telling your manager? What matters more—being available or being entrepreneurial? And so on. Actually ask those questions; don't just assume you know the answers. Without that information, you might get paranoid that you're seen as a slacker or actually not doing enough—and way, way overcompensate.

Develop and maintain your network. Justin Mass, a senior learning technologist at Adobe, volunteers for cross-functional projects that increase his exposure to his HQ colleagues. He's worked to become known as a guy who raises his hand before being asked, and that's helped him create strong connections throughout the company.

If possible, have your company occasionally fly you to HQ or other key offices. Fill your time with meetings—breakfast, lunch, and dinner—to build relationships. Ask people about themselves and their work—you can glean a lot about what's going on in the organization and where the opportunities are. (Keep it professional, of course. This isn't the time to have a few too many beers or complain about your manager.) You'll be exhausted after all these meetings, but you'll have made the most of your short amount of time onsite.

If you're a new hire, you'll need to build a foundation: Ask for a visit to the home office to put names to faces, get a sense of the culture in the building, and get face time by attending a meeting or two. But not too soon! For your first few months on the job, you'll be learning many things, so time your visit (if you can make just one) for when you're in a position of having good questions to ask, not just passively absorbing information. When you do make your trip, introduce yourself to people you'll need to interact with. Find out from team members who else you should reach out to, and ask if they'd be willing to help you connect.

It's virtually impossible to navigate a company's spoken and unspoken "rules" without a guide. You can't simply assume that the culture is casual because, say, dogs are allowed in the office on Fridays. That same company might be rigid about protocol. It takes a little digging to figure out which people in the organization get things done. Have someone in the know walk you through the org chart and explain the company's circles of influence to you. Ask pointed questions: Who is the right contact for that group? What works best here—e-mail, phone calls, or IM? Are there informal power brokers I should make contact with? That kind of thing.

Start Skyping

Adobe's Mass is the only member of his team who works entirely from a home office, yet he collaborates with colleagues in California and India every day. Videoconferencing has been critical to his success. Every chance to be seen on video, he says, is a chance to improve your visibility with your team. You become more than a disembodied voice.

While his company has installed high-end video technology in his home office, he notes that Skype, which is free to anyone, also does the job. Of course, being visible also makes you more accountable. "I think of every video meeting as an opportunity for my team to see me in action," Mass says. "I have to bring my A game."

He actually thinks like a movie director shooting a scene when he considers how he's going to be perceived by his colleagues on the other end of the camera. He dresses professionally and keeps his desk clean. He's even painted his walls the same neutral manila as those at headquarters so his workspace doesn't "look like some strange foreign office." He makes a point to sit forward in his chair, engaged, as if he were at the same conference table. He looks at the camera. Never pushes the mute button and just listens in. Never multitasks.

Mass's advice for others wanting to make videoconferencing work? Do a trial video chat with a friend. Study the thumbnail image of yourself on screen, and ask your friend for feedback. "See how your colleagues will see you," he says. "What's in the background? How are you showing yourself? Are you slumping in your chair? Are you taking notes?"

If your colleagues aren't ready for Skype, be thoughtful about the conference call. Ask your manager what's expected of you (Am I just getting briefed? Am I part of the brainstorming team? Do you need me to report on what I've been up to?). Once I was caught off guard on a conference call by a manager asking us each to "go around the horn" and give updates. What he *really* meant was, "If there's anything of burning importance, now's your chance." But absent any body language or other visual cues to put his request in context, I panicked and assumed I needed to show how productive I'd been. When I finished my monologue, a few long minutes later, it was obvious I'd gotten it wrong, and we swiftly moved on to other topics. If you don't have a chance to clarify expectations in advance, it may be better to listen quietly and then contribute follow-up thoughts by e-mail or phone. Ask your manager to occasionally put you on the agenda to discuss what you're working on, share your observations, or report on a project.

Since remote colleagues and partners are likely to be a permanent feature of any growing company, it's important to manage these relationships well. And it's worth the effort. If you're a hiring manager, who says the right person for the job you've posted lives within driving distance? And if you're a remote worker, you can get a lot of work done, in fewer hours than your HQ colleagues, if you use your time wisely.

It's possible to make off-site work relationships both productive and powerful—I've found that some of my remote colleagues over the years have been great allies and sounding boards. But the key to success, on both sides of the relationship, is utter transparency and thinking *ahead* about what your colleagues most need from you.

Karen Dillon is the former editor of *Harvard Business Review* and a coauthor, with Clayton Christensen and James Allworth, of the book *How Will You Measure Your Life?* (HarperBusiness, 2012).

A Smarter Way to Network

A summary of the full-length HBR article by **Rob Cross** *and* **Robert Thomas,** *highlighting key ideas.*

THE IDEA IN BRIEF

To maximize your and your team's performance, you need resources, information, and expertise from people across your organization. They don't report to you, but they can make—or break—your project.

So you must influence them. How? Build a better network, using these steps:

1. **Analyze:** Identify the benefits each of your existing network connections now provides. Does one person give you valuable information? Does another have expertise you need but lack?

Reprint #R1107P

2. **De-layer:** Weed out connections that aren't helping you, such as people who burn too much of your time.

3. **Diversify:** Fill the fresh openings in your network with people who can deliver the additional benefits you and your team need to accomplish your work.

Construct a strong network, and you'll have a wider, richer web of connections to draw on when the next crisis or opportunity lands on your desk.

THE IDEA IN PRACTICE

When you need help from colleagues up, down, and across the organization, every network choice you make matters. Use these steps to make your selections:

1. Analyze

Identify the individuals currently in your network.

Determine:

- **Where they're located.** Are they on your team? In your unit? Outside your organization? Are they higher-ups? Peers? Frontline workers? You want a diverse but select web of high-quality relationships with people who hail from several different spheres and levels in your organization.

- **What benefits they're providing.** Do they offer information, expertise, or best practices that can help you lead projects more effectively? Are they formally powerful people who can provide political "juice"? For instance, can they remind lazy members of a task force you're on how important their project is to the organization? Are they informally influential people who can win you needed support among the rank-and-file?

2. De-layer

Make tough decisions about relationships to back away from. Eliminate or minimize contact with people who sap your energy or offer benefits that others in your network already provide. By de-layering, you make room for people who can help you complete projects.

3. Diversify

Fill the new openings in your network with the right people, using this technique:

- Articulate three business goals you plan to achieve this year.

- List the people who could help you reach these goals—and how. Is it their expertise? Their control over resources? Their political support?

- Actively build relationships with these individuals.

    Example: Joe, an investment banker, needed to expand his global client pool. First he identified counterparts in his company's Asian and European operations who had relationships with clients he had targeted. Then he scheduled regular calls with his colleagues to synchronize their selling efforts. In some cases, these calls helped him identify opportunities he could pitch proactively, such as potential clients who were interested in his department's offerings. In others, the calls helped him and his peers appear more coordinated when their bank was competing against other banks for the same clients.

One of the happiest, most successful executives we know is a woman named Deb. She works at a major technology company and runs a global business unit that has more than 7,000 employees. When you ask her how she rose to the top and why she enjoys her job, her answer is simple: people. She points to her boss, the CEO, a mentor who "always has her back"; Steve, the head of a complementary business, with whom she has monthly brainstorming lunches and occasional gripe sessions; and Tom, a protégé to whom she has delegated responsibility for a large portion of her division. Outside the company, Deb's circle includes her counterparts in three strategic partnerships, who inspire her with new ideas; Sheila, a former colleague, now in a different industry, who gives her candid feedback; and her husband, Bob, an executive at a philanthropic organization. She also has close relationships with her fellow volunteers in a program for at-risk high school students and the members of her tennis group and book club.

This is Deb's social network (the real-world kind, not the virtual kind), and it has helped her career a lot. But not because the group is large or full of high-powered contacts. Her network is effective because it both supports and challenges her. Deb's relationships help her gain influence, broaden her expertise, learn new skills, and find purpose and balance. Deb values and nurtures them. "Make friends so that you have friends when you need friends" is her motto.

"My current role is really a product of a relationship I formed over a decade ago that came back to me at the right time," she explains. "People may chalk it up to luck, but I think more often than not luck happens through networks where people give first and are authentic in all they do."

Over the past 15 years, we've worked with many executives like Deb, at more than 300 companies. What began as organizational research—helping management teams understand and capitalize on the formal and informal social networks of their employees—has since metamorphosed into personal programs, which teach individual executives to increase their effectiveness by leveraging their networks.

The old adage "It's not what you know, it's who you know" is true. But it's more nuanced than that. In spite of what most self-help books say, network size doesn't usually matter. In fact, we've found that individuals who simply know a lot of people are less likely to achieve standout performance, because they're spread too thin. Political animals with lots of connections to corporate and industry leaders don't win the day, either. Yes, it's important to know powerful people, but if they account for too much of your network, your peers and subordinates often perceive you to be overly self-interested, and you may lose support as a result.

The data we've collected point to a different model

for networking. The executives who consistently rank in the top 20% of their companies in both performance and well-being have diverse but select networks like Deb's—made up of high-quality relationships with people who come from several different spheres and from up and down the corporate hierarchy. These high performers, we have found, tap into six critical kinds of connections, which enhance their careers and lives in a variety of ways.

Through our work advising individual managers, we've also identified a four-step process that will help any executive develop this kind of network. But first, let's take a look at some common networking mistakes.

Getting It Wrong

Many people take a misguided approach to networking. They go astray by building imbalanced networks, pursuing the wrong kind of relationships, or leveraging relationships ineffectively. (See the sidebar "Are You Networking Impaired?") These people might remain successful for a time, but often they will hit a plateau or see their career derailed because their networks couldn't prompt or support a critical transition.

Consider Dan, the chief information officer of one of the world's largest life-sciences organizations. He was under constant pressure to find new technologies that would spur innovation and speed the drug commercialization process at his company, and he needed a network that would help him. Unfortunately, more than 70% of his trusted advisers were in the unit he had worked in before becoming CIO. Not only did they reinforce his bias toward certain solutions and vendors, but they lacked the outside knowledge he needed. "I had started to mistake friendship, trust, and accessibility for real expertise in new domains," he told us. "This didn't mean I was going to dump these people, as they played important roles for me in other ways. But I needed to be more targeted in who I let influence my thinking."

Another overarching mistake we often see in executives' networks is an imbalance between connections that promote career advancement and those that promote engagement and satisfaction. Numerous studies have shown that happier executives are higher-performing ones.

Take Tim, the director of a large practice area at a leading professional services firm. On the surface he was doing well, but job stress had taken its toll. He was 40 pounds overweight, with alarmingly high cholesterol and blood sugar levels, and prone to extreme mood swings. When things went well at work, he was happy; when they didn't, he wasn't pleasant to be around. In fact, Tim's wife finally broke down and told him she thought he had become a career-obsessed jerk and needed to get other interests. With her encouragement, he joined Habitat for Humanity and started rowing with their daughter. As a result, his social network expanded to include people with different perspectives and values, who helped him focus on more healthful and fulfilling pursuits. "As I spent more time with different groups, what I cared about diversified," he says. "Physically, I'm in much better shape and probably staved off a heart attack. But I think I'm a better leader, too, in that I think about problems more broadly, and I'm more resilient. Our peer feedback systems are

ARE YOU NETWORKING IMPAIRED?

In our work, we have identified six common managerial types who get stuck in three kinds of network traps. Do any of the descriptions below fit you?

The wrong structure

THE FORMALIST focuses too heavily on his company's official hierarchy, missing out on the efficiencies and opportunities that come from informal connections.

THE OVERLOADED MANAGER has so much contact with colleagues and external ties that she becomes a bottleneck to progress and burns herself out.

The wrong relationships

THE DISCONNECTED EXPERT sticks with people who keep him focused on safe, existing competencies,

also clearly indicating that people are more committed to the new me."

Getting It Right

To understand more about what makes an effective network, let's look again at Deb. She has a small set of core contacts—14 people she really relies on. Effective core networks typically range in size from 12 to 18 people. But what really matters is structure: Core connections must rather than those who push him to build new skills.

THE BIASED LEADER relies on advisers much like herself (same functional background, location, or values), who reinforce her biases, when she should instead seek outsiders to prompt more fully informed decisions.

The wrong behavior

THE SUPERFICIAL NETWORKER engages in surface-level interaction with as many people as possible, mistakenly believing that a bigger network is a better one.

THE CHAMELEON changes his interests, values, and personality to match those of whatever subgroup is his audience, and winds up being disconnected from every group.

bridge smaller, more-diverse kinds of groups and cross hierarchical, organizational, functional, and geographic lines. Core relationships should result in more learning, less bias in decision making, and greater personal growth and balance. The people in your inner circle should also model positive behaviors, because if those around you are enthusiastic, authentic, and generous, you will be, too.

More specifically, our data show that high performers have strong ties to:

1. people who offer them new information or expertise, including internal or external clients, who increase their market awareness; peers in other functions, divisions, or geographies, who share best practices; and contacts in other industries, who inspire innovation;

2. formally powerful people, who provide mentoring, sense-making, political support, and resources; and informally powerful people, who offer influence, help coordinating projects, and support among the rank and file; and

3. people who give them developmental feedback, challenge their decisions, and push them to be better. At an early career stage, an employee might get this from a boss or customers; later, it tends to come from coaches, trusted colleagues, or a spouse.

Meanwhile, the most satisfied executives have ties to:

1. people who provide personal support, such as colleagues who help them get back on track when they're having a bad day or friends with whom they can just be themselves;

2. people who add a sense of purpose or worth, such as bosses and customers who validate their work, and family members and other stakeholders who show them work has a broader meaning; and

3. people who promote their work/life balance, holding them accountable for activities that improve their physical health (such as sports), mental engagement (such as hobbies or educational classes), or spiritual well-being (music, religion, art, or volunteer work).

How does one create such a varied network? We recommend a four-point action plan: analyze, de-layer, diversify, and capitalize.

Analyze

Start by looking at the individuals in your network. Where are they located—are they within your team, your unit, or your company, or outside your organization? What benefits do your interactions with them provide? How energizing are those interactions?

The last question is an important one. Energizers bring out the best in everyone around them, and our data show that having them in your network is a strong predictor of success over time. These people aren't necessarily extroverted or charismatic. They're people who always see opportunities, even in challenging situations, and create room for others to meaningfully contribute. Good energizers are trustworthy and committed to principles larger than their self-interest, and they enjoy other people. "De-energizers," by contrast, are quick to point out obstacles, critique people rather than ideas, are inflexible in their thinking, fail to create opportunities, miss commitments, and don't show concern for others.

FOUR STEPS TO BUILDING A BETTER NETWORK

Analyze

- Identify the people in your network and what you get out of interacting with them

De-layer

- Make some hard decisions to back away from redundant and energy-sapping relationships

Diversify

- Build your network out with the right kind of people: energizers who will help you achieve your goals

Capitalize

- Make sure you're using your contacts as effectively as you can

Unfortunately, energy-sapping interactions have more impact than energizing ones—up to seven times as much, according to one study. And our own research suggests that roughly 90% of anxiety at work is created by 5% of one's network—the people who sap energy.

Next, classify your relationships by the benefits they provide. Generally, benefits fall into one of six basic categories: information, political support and influence, personal development, personal support and energy, a sense of purpose or worth, and work/life balance. It's important to have people who provide each kind of benefit in your network. Categorizing your relationships will give you a clearer idea of whether your network is extending your abilities or keeping you stuck. You'll see where you have holes and redundancies and which people you depend on too much—or not enough.

Let's use Joe, a rising star in an investment bank, as a case study. He had 24 close advisers—on the surface, a more than healthy number. But many of the people he relied on were from his own department and frequently relied on one another. If he eliminated those redundancies, his network shrank to five people. After giving it some thought and observing his peers' networks, he realized he was missing links with several important types of people: colleagues focused on financial offerings outside his own products, who could help him deliver broader financial solutions to customers; coworkers in different geographies—particularly London and Asia—who could enhance his ability to sell to global clients; and board-level relationships at key accounts, who could make client introductions and influence purchasing decisions. His insularity was limiting his options and hurting his chances of promotion to managing director. He realized he would need to focus on cultivating a network rather than allowing it to organically arise from the day-to-day demands of his work.

De-layer

Once you've analyzed your network, you need to make some hard decisions about which relationships to back away from. First, look at eliminating or minimizing contact with people who sap you of energy or promote unhealthful behaviors. You can do this by reshaping your role to avoid them, devoting less time to them, working to change their behavior, or reframing your reactions so that you don't dwell on the interactions.

John, an academic, realized that two university administrators in his network were causing him a great deal of anxiety. This had so soured his view of his school that he was considering leaving. He therefore decided to devote less time to projects and committees that would involve the negative contacts and to avoid dwelling on any sniping comments they subjected him to. Within a year he was much more productive and happy. "By shifting my role and how I reacted to the idiots, I turned a negative situation around," John says. "In hindsight it was an obvious move—rather than leave a place I loved—but emotions can spiral on you in ways you don't recognize."

The next step is to ask yourself which of the six categories have too many people in them. Early-stage leaders, for example, tend to focus too much on information and not enough on personal development and might want to shed some of the contacts who give them the former to make more time for those who give them the latter.

Beyond this, consider which individuals—and types of people as determined by function, hierarchy, or geography—have too much of you, and why. Is the cause structural, in that work procedures require you to be involved? Or is your own behavior causing the imbalance? What can you change to rectify the situation? Too often we see leaders fail because they accept or create too many collaborative demands.

Paul, the head of research in a consumer products company, had a network of almost 70 people just at work.

But he got many complaints from people who said they needed greater access to him. His productivity, and his unit's, was suffering. When he analyzed his network, he realized that he was missing "people and initiatives one or two levels out." To address this, he decided to delegate— stepping away from interactions that didn't require his presence and cultivating "go to" stand-ins in certain areas of expertise. He also changed his leadership style from extraordinarily accessible to helpful but more removed, which encouraged subordinates to solve their own problems by connecting with people around him. "As a leader you can find yourself in this bubble of activity where you feel like a lot is happening moving from meeting to meeting," Paul says. "You can actually start to thrive on this in some ways. I had to move past this for us to be effective as a unit and so that I could be more forward-thinking."

Diversify

Now that you've created room in your network, you need to fill it with the right people. Simple tools like work sheets can help you get started. For example, you might make a list of the six categories of relationships and think about colleagues who could fill the holes you have in each. Remember to focus on positive, energetic, selfless people, and be sure to ask people inside and outside your network for recommendations.

You should also think about how you could connect your network to your professional and personal goals. Here's another simple exercise: Write down three specific business results you hope to achieve over the next year (such as doubling sales or winning an Asia-based client) and then list the people (by name or general role) who could help you with them, thanks to their expertise, control over resources, or ability to provide political support. Joe, the investment banker, identified counterparts in the Asian and European operations of his company who had relationships with the clients he was focused on and then scheduled regular calls with them to coordinate efforts. "In a couple of cases this helped me identify opportunities I could pitch proactively. In others it just helped us appear more coordinated when we were competing against other banks," he says. One of the big challenges for Paul, the consumer products executive, was managing a new facility and line of innovation in China. Because none of his trusted advisers had ever even been to that country, he reached out to the head of R&D at a major life-sciences organization that had undertaken a similar effort.

Capitalize

Last, make sure you're using your contacts as effectively as you can. Are there people you rely on in one sphere, such as political support, that you could also use to fill a need in another, such as personal development? Could you get more out of some relationships if you put more energy into them? Our research shows, for instance, that high performers at all levels tend to use their information contacts to gain other benefits, such as new ideas. Reciprocal relationships also tend to be more fruitful; the most successful leaders always look for ways to give more to their contacts.

Alan, a top executive at a global insurance company, realized that although he had a good network, he was still making decisions in relative isolation. He failed to elicit insights from others and, as a result, wasn't making enough progress toward his goals. So he started inviting his more-junior contacts, who were informal opinion leaders in his company, to lunch and asking them open-ended questions. These conversations led him to streamline decision making and uncover innovation deep within the firm's hierarchy. "When I met with one lady, I was stunned at a great new product idea she had been pushing for months," Alan says. "But she hadn't been able to get the right people to listen. I was able to step in and help make things happen. To me the right way to be tapping into people is in this exploratory way—whether it is about strategic insights or just how they think I'm doing on some aspect of my job. That's how I get to new ways of thinking and doing things, and I know it makes me much more effective than people who are smarter than me."

A network constructed using this four-point model will build on itself over time. In due course, it will ensure that the best opportunities, ideas, and talent come your way.

Rob Cross (robcross@virginia.edu) is an associate professor at the University of Virginia's McIntire School of Commerce. **Robert Thomas** is the executive director of the Accenture Institute for High Performance.

How to Deal with Office Politics

by Linda A. Hill and Kent Lineback

"I don't care who they are. I won't buddy up to people I don't like and respect just because I want something from them."

These are the words of a *Fortune* 500 senior manager, but we hear similar comments from managers at all levels, in all types of companies. Perhaps you feel the same way.

Do you dismiss most of the give-and-take in organizations as "office politics"—ego-driven, manipulative, dysfunctional game playing? Do you tend to focus on your own group and deal with others only when you like them personally or the immediate work requires it? If this describes your approach, you're probably making yourself and your group less effective than you should be.

Every organization has a political environment—that is, one where human relationships matter—and yours is no exception. To obtain the resources, influence, and at-

Adapted from content posted on hbr.org on November 2, 2011

tention you and your group need, you must be able to function in such a setting by actively engaging others, whether you like them or not.

The good news: You can do that without succumbing to mean and self-interested tactics. The secret is to *build ongoing relationships for mutual advantage.*

Here's how to navigate your political environment positively and professionally:

- **Focus on the good of the enterprise.** A big-picture view will help you do what's best for your group. Recognize your interdependence with other units, and consider how your goals and theirs align. If customer service reps say a forthcoming product will require a lot of extra support, get their input on ways to make it more user-friendly. They'll be happier with fewer calls to answer, and you'll have a better product to sell. You'll become allies, without even a hint of schmoozing. And don't be afraid to share customers with other divisions. It shows that you're a team player—and your customers will appreciate the seamless service.

- **Keep disagreements professional.** Focus on issues, not personalities. Suppose you work at an insurance company, for example, and people in the underwriting department resist your plan to offer a new type of homeowner's policy. Assume they have legitimate concerns and try to understand and accommodate them. Accusing colleagues of "not knowing the market" or being "stuck in the last century" certainly won't win them over or allow you to find an approach that meets everyone's needs. And complaining about them behind their backs will surely come back to bite you.

- **Share information.** When it comes to information, you get what you give, and what you know depends on who you know. Say your IT director has just filled three positions that have been open for months. Alert your colleagues in product development so they can update their list of tech priorities. If you look for ways to make their lives easier, they'll probably return the favor when they get an inside scoop that affects your work.

- **Relay good news about your team members.** They'll likely appreciate the public recognition, and it'll help the rest of the organization see the value they add. Did your group finish a critical project early *and* under budget? Send an e-mail to managers you work with closely, and copy the individuals whose praises you're singing. Don't assume that everyone will automatically notice your group's success. If you don't mention it, who will?

- **Above all, focus your relationships on what's best for "us."** If you want an exception to your company's pricing policy and need a colleague's help, identify her goals and find a way you can support her and her group, too. And talk to her about what you want to achieve; perhaps there's a way to serve both your purposes simultaneously. Let "connect and collaborate" be your mantra.

We're not saying that organizations are ideal worlds where everyone always wants the best for everyone else. They're often maelstroms of conflicting goals, divergent interests, and fierce struggles for scarce resources. And organizational bullies *do* exist. They play games and pick fights. They define their success by the interpersonal battles they win, not the results they accomplish for the organization. How do you deal with them? Not by hiding.

Bullies are actually a key reason *not* to withdraw to your own corner of the organization. You can counter their tactics with the help of allies. If someone spreads half-truths about you or quotes you or your people out of context, it's much easier to set the record straight if you've developed influence through strong relationships.

Raise the bar by conducting yourself according to standards that matter to you. Be honest, courteous, and dependable—no matter how others act. If you propose an idea that someone belittles, don't retaliate by pointing out flaws in his idea. That just creates a poisonous atmosphere. Instead, try to get at what's behind the aggressive behavior. Maybe that person feels threatened by you. Look for ways to lower his defenses—ask for his advice, invite him to brainstorming sessions, and so on. You may find that he's suddenly more collaborative and less combative.

Linda A. Hill is the Wallace Brett Donham Professor of Business Administration and faculty chair of the Leadership Initiative at Harvard Business School. Now a writer and executive coach, **Kent Lineback** spent many years as a manager and an executive in business and government. They are the coauthors of *Being the Boss: The 3 Imperatives for Becoming a Great Leader* (Harvard Business Review Press, 2011).

Make Your Enemies Your Allies

by Brian Uzzi and Shannon Dunlap

John Clendenin was fresh out of business school in 1984 when he took on his first managerial position, in Xerox's parts and supply division. He was an obvious outsider: young, African-American, and a former Marine, whose pink shirts and brown suits stood out amid the traditional gray and black attire of his new colleagues. "I was strikingly different," he recalls. And yet his new role required him to lead a team including employees who had been with Xerox for decades.

One of his direct reports was Tom Gunning, a 20-year company veteran who believed Clendenin's job should have gone to him, not to a younger, nontechnical newcomer. Gunning also had a cadre of pals on the team. As a result, Clendenin's first days were filled with strained

---

Reprint #R1205K

smiles and behind-the-back murmurs. Though he wasn't looking for adversaries, "I knew these guys were discontented about me coming in," Clendenin remembers.

He was right to be wary. Anyone who has faced a rival at work—a colleague threatened by your skills, a superior unwilling to acknowledge your good ideas, or a subordinate who undermines you—knows such dynamics can prove catastrophic for your career, and for your group or organization. When those with formal or informal power are fighting you, you may find it impossible to accomplish—or get credit for—any meaningful work. And even if you have the upper hand, an antagonistic relationship inevitably casts a cloud over you and your team, sapping energy, stymieing progress, and distracting group members from their goals.

Because rivalries can be so destructive, it's not enough to simply ignore, sidestep, or attempt to contain them. Instead, effective leaders turn rivals into collaborators— strengthening their positions, their networks, and their careers in the process. Think of these relationships not as chronic illnesses you have to endure but as wounds that must be treated in order for you to lead a healthy work life.

Here we share a method, called the 3Rs, for efficiently and effectively turning your adversaries into your allies. If you execute each step correctly, you will develop new "connective tissue" within your organization, boosting your ability to broker knowledge and drive fresh thinking. The method is drawn from our own inductive case studies—including interviews with business leaders such as John Clendenin, who agreed to let us tell his story in this article—and from empirical research conducted by Brian and others investigating the physiology of the brain, the sociology of relationships, and the psychology of influence.

Emotions and Trust

Many well-intentioned efforts to reverse rivalries fail in large part because of the complex way trust operates in these relationships. Research shows that trust is based on both reason and emotion. If the emotional orientation toward a person is negative—typically because of a perceived threat—then reason will be twisted to align with those negative feelings. This is why feuds can stalemate trust: New facts and arguments, no matter how credible and logical, may be seen as ploys to dupe the other side. This effect is not just psychological; it is physiological. When we experience negative emotions, blood recedes from the thinking part of the brain, the cerebral cortex, and rushes to its oldest and most involuntary part, the "reptilian" stem, crippling the intake of new information.

Most executives who decide they want to reverse a rivalry will, quite understandably, turn to reason, presenting incentives for trustworthy collaboration. But in these situations, the "emotional brain" must be managed before adversaries can understand evidence and be persuaded.

When John Clendenin looked at Tom Gunning at Xerox, he immediately saw grounds for a strong partnership beyond a perfunctory subordinate-superior relationship. Gunning had 20 years' worth of organizational and technical knowledge, and contacts around the company, but he lacked the leadership skills and vision that Clendenin possessed. Conversely, Clendenin understood management but needed Gunning's expertise and connections to successfully navigate his new company. Unfortunately, Gunning's emotions were getting in the way. Clendenin needed to employ the 3Rs.

Redirection

Step 1 is to redirect your rival's negative emotions so that they are channeled away from you. Clendenin decided to have a one-on-one meeting with Gunning, but not in his office, because that would only remind Gunning of the promotion he'd lost. Instead, he found out where Gunning liked to eat and took him there for lunch. "I was letting him know that I understood his worth," Clendenin says of this contextual redirection.

He followed this with a plain statement of redirection, telling Gunning that a third entity beyond the control of both men was the root cause of their situation. "I didn't put you in this position," Clendenin said. "Xerox put us both in this position."

Many executives scoff when they first hear this story, believing Clendenin's actions to be too transparent. But redirection doesn't have to be hidden. With stage magic, for example, audience members understand that redirection is happening, but that doesn't lessen their acceptance or spoil the payoff of the technique. Other personal interactions work similarly. For instance, we accept flattery even if we recognize it as such.

Another common redirection tactic is to introduce a discussion of things you and your rival have in common, or casually portray a source of tension—a particular initiative, employee, or event—in a more favorable light. It sounds obvious. But redirection will shift negative emotions away from you and lay the groundwork for Step 2: reciprocity.

Reciprocity

The essential principle here is to *give before you ask.* Undoing a negative tie begins with giving up something of value rather than asking for a "fair trade." If you give and then ask for something right away in return, you don't establish a relationship; you carry out a transaction.

When done correctly, reciprocity is like priming the pump. In the old days, pumps required lots of exertion to produce any water. You had to repeatedly work a lever to eliminate a vacuum in the line before water could flow. But if you poured a small bucket of water into the line first, the vacuum was quickly eliminated, enabling the water to flow with less effort. Reciprocity with a rival works in much the same way.

Reflect carefully on *what* you should give and, ideally, choose something that requires little effort from the other party to reciprocate. Clendenin moved from redirection to reciprocity at the lunch by promising to support Gunning's leadership development and future advancement at Xerox. But, recognizing that mere promises of future returns wouldn't be enough to spark collaboration, he also offered Gunning something concrete: the chance to attend executive-level meetings. This was of immediate value, not a distant, murky benefit. Gunning could gain visibility, credibility, and connections.

The arrangement also ensured reciprocity. Gunning's presence at the meetings furnished Clendenin with on-hand technical expertise and organizational knowledge while giving him "reputation points" with Gunning's contacts. Thus, his offer created the purest form of reciprocity; if Gunning attended the meetings, Clendenin would never have to explicitly request a quid pro quo.

Reciprocity involves considering ways that you can immediately fulfill a rival's need or reduce a pain point. Live up to your end of the bargain first, but figure out a way to ensure a return from your rival without the person's feeling that pressure. Another example comes from Brian's colleague Adam Galinsky, who advises leaders in contentious restructurings and business closings to generate goodwill among outgoing employees by offering professional references or placements at other companies as long as the employees continue to meet or exceed expectations until their office closes. The employees see immediate value, and although they don't consciously pay back the organization, the firm nonetheless benefits by maintaining continuity in its workforce until the scheduled closure.

Similarly, a colleague who helps an adversary complete a project, or a subordinate who stays overtime to finish a task for a difficult boss, not only helps that individual but can reap rewards when other teammates or superiors benefit from that effort, too. Here the judicious giving before asking sets a foundation for reciprocity with third parties, whose buy-in can positively assist in reshaping the adversarial relationship. (See the sidebar "Rivalries Don't Exist in a Vacuum.")

Rationality

Step 3, rationality, establishes the expectations of the fledgling relationship you've built using the previous

RIVALRIES DON'T EXIST IN A VACUUM

Even when a leader executes the 3Rs flawlessly to end a rivalry, his work isn't necessarily done.

That's because the relationship is often about more than just the two individuals. We all know people who seek to play to their advantage antagonism between others; some third parties might even view a blossoming partnership with trepidation or envy, triggering new negative emotions and rivalries.

You can head off this problem, as Clendenin did, by framing your work as beneficial not just to you and your adversary but to the whole organization, which makes the reversal of rivalry in everyone's interest. When Clendenin brought Gunning into those executive-level meetings, he made it clear that Gunning was going to be a "poster child" for a new age at Xerox, in which talented, long-term employees could find new paths to leadership in a time of corporate transition. Even if the conflictmongers didn't care about Clendenin's and Gunning's success, it would be far more difficult for them to sabotage an effort that was obviously good for the company.

steps so that your efforts don't come off as dishonest or as ineffective pandering. What would have happened if Clendenin had left the lunch without explaining how he wanted to work with Gunning going forward? Gunning might have begun to second-guess his new boss's intentions and resumed his adversarial stance. If a rival is worried about the other shoe's dropping, his emotional unease can undermine the trust you've built.

To employ rationality, Clendenin told Gunning that he needed him, or someone like him, to reach his goals at Xerox. This made it clear that he saw Gunning as a valuable, but not indispensable, partner. Another, softer approach might have involved Clendenin's giving Gunning "the right of first refusal" to collaborate with him, making the offer seem special while judiciously indicating that there were others who could step in. Just to be clear, Clendenin was not asking Gunning for a specific favor in exchange for the one he'd granted in Step 2. He was simply saying that he wanted him to become an ally.

Clendenin also reinforced the connection between the three steps by making his offer time-limited, which raised the perception of the value of the deal without changing its content. He told Gunning he needed an answer before they left the restaurant. "I needed to nip this in the bud," Clendenin recalls. "He knew I didn't care if we sat in that restaurant until midnight if we had to."

When rationality follows redirection and reciprocity, it should push your adversary into considering the situation from a reasoned standpoint, fully comprehending the expectations and benefits, and recognizing that he is looking at a valued opportunity that could be lost. Most people are highly motivated to avoid a loss, which complements their desire to gain something. Rationality is like offering medicine after a spoonful of sugar: It ensures that you're getting the benefit of the shifted negative emotions, and any growing positive ones, which would otherwise diffuse over time.

And it avoids the ambiguity that clouds expectations and feedback when flattery and favors come one day, and demands the next.

Of course, Clendenin and Gunning did not walk out of the restaurant as full-blown collaborators. But both accepted that they should give each other the benefit of the doubt. Over the following weeks, this new mind-set allowed them to work as allies, a process that deepened trust and resource-sharing in a self-reinforcing cycle. So a potentially debilitating rivalry was transformed into a healthy working relationship and, in time, a strong partnership. Several years later, when Clendenin moved to another Xerox unit, he nominated Gunning as his replacement—and Gunning excelled in the position. The foundation for that remarkable shift had been established during the span of a single lunch.

Adapting the 3Rs

A key advantage of the 3Rs is that the method can work to reverse all kinds of rivalries, including those with a peer or a superior. Later in Clendenin's tenure at Xerox, he noticed an inefficiency in the company's inventory systems. At the time, Xerox was made up of semiautonomous international units that stockpiled excess inventory to avoid shortages. Clendenin proposed that the units instead share their inventories through an intrafirm network that would improve resource use and lower carrying costs for the company as a whole. Although the idea was objectively good for Xerox, it threatened the power of some unit vice presidents, so when Clendenin floated his idea, they shot it down.

WHAT IF THE 3RS FAIL?

The 3Rs are effective, but they aren't a guarantee. What should you do if the strategy isn't working?

Strive for collaboration indirectly—for example, by working well with a third party whom your rival trusts. A common ally can highlight to him the benefits of working with you.

Remember that timing matters. People in power need a reason to interact. This was certainly the case with John Clendenin's inventory-management pitch to the Xerox VPs: At first rebuffed, he was able to refloat his idea when the CEO called for a new strategy.

Recognize when to look elsewhere. Sometimes the effort needed to reverse a rivalry is so great, and the returns so low, for you and your company that you're better off deploying the same resources in another relationship.

A short time later, however, following an unexpected announcement by the CEO that the company needed better asset management, Clendenin found a way to reintroduce his proposal to the VPs. Because he knew they viewed him as an unwelcome challenger—or rival—he used the 3Rs.

His first move was to redirect their negative emotions away from him by planning a lunch for them at the regional office and serving them himself. This showed deference. He also presented himself not as an individual pushing a proposal but as someone who could expedite organizational change, shifting the reference point of his rivals' tension. "With all of those egos and personalities, I never said, 'This is my idea,'" Clendenin recalls. "I always said 'we.'"

Applying the reciprocity principle of give before you ask, he requested nothing from them at the meeting. Instead, he facilitated a discussion about the CEO-led initiative. Inventory management was, unsurprisingly, a problem cited by many of the VPs, and Clendenin's facilitation brought that to light. He then took on the luster of the person who had illuminated a generic problem, rather than someone who wanted to lessen the VPs' autonomy.

That allowed him to present the rationality of his original idea. All of a sudden, it looked like an opportunity, rather than a threat, to the formerly antagonistic group. Clendenin indicated that he would be willing to coordinate a new system more cheaply than anyone else in the market could offer, while also noting that he might not have time to do so in the future, which raised the perceived value of his offer. The VPs agreed to execute the plan in stages and put Clendenin in charge. The initiative grew in small but steady steps, eventually saving Xerox millions. Equally important, Clendenin's embrace by his rivals positioned him as a broker in the company and burnished his reputation as an institution builder.

John Clendenin understood that rivalries help no one; indeed, success often depends on not just neutralizing your foes but turning them into collaborators. By using the 3Rs to build trust in his network, Clendenin made sure everyone in his network thrived—including himself, Gunning, their team, the VPs, and Xerox—forming the basis for long-term ties and shared success. Years later, Clendenin started his own international logistics company. His partner in this new endeavor was his old rival, Tom Gunning, and the lead investors were none other than the unit VPs from Xerox who had once shot down his ideas.

———

Brian Uzzi is the Richard L. Thomas Professor of Leadership and Organizational Change at Northwestern's Kellogg School of Management and the codirector of the Northwestern Institute on Complex Systems (NICO). **Shannon Dunlap** is a journalist and writer based in New York City.

The authors' research was supported by grants from the National Science Foundation (OCI-0838564—VOSS) and the U.S. Army Research Laboratory's Network Science Collaborative Technology Alliance (W911NF-09-2-0053).

The Necessary Art of Persuasion

A summary of the full-length HBR article by **Jay A. Conger,** *highlighting key ideas.*

THE IDEA IN BRIEF

When you're operating outside clear reporting lines, your colleagues may not immediately see why they should collaborate with you. That's when your powers of persuasion come into play. It's not manipulation. Effective persuasion is a learning and negotiating process for leading your colleagues to a *shared solution* to a problem.

Reprint #4258

THE IDEA IN PRACTICE

The process of persuasion has four steps:

1. **Establish credibility.** Your credibility grows out of two sources: **expertise** and **relationships**. If you have a history of well-informed, sound judgment, your colleagues will trust your expertise. If you've demonstrated that you can work in the best interest of others, your peers will have confidence in your relationships.

   If you're weak on the expertise side, bolster your position by:

   - Learning more through formal and informal education—for example, conversations with in-house experts

   - Hiring recognized outside experts

   - Launching pilot projects

     Example: Two developers at Microsoft envisioned a controversial new software product, but both were technology novices. By working closely with technical experts and market testing a prototype, they persuaded management that the new product was ideally suited to the average computer user. It sold half a million units.

To fill in the relationship gap, try:

- Meeting one-on-one with key people

- Involving like-minded coworkers who have good support with your audience

2. **Frame goals on common ground.** Tangibly describe the benefits of your position. The fastest way to get a child to the grocery store is to point out the lollipops by the cash register. That's not deception—it's persuasion. When no shared advantages are apparent, adjust your position.

> *Example:* An ad agency executive persuaded skeptical fast-food franchisees to support headquarters' new price discounts. She cited reliable research showing how the pricing scheme improved franchisees' profits. They supported the new plan unanimously.

3. **Vividly reinforce your position.** Ordinary evidence won't do. Make numerical data more compelling with examples, stories, and metaphors that have an emotional impact.

> *Example:* The founder of Mary Kay Cosmetics made a speech comparing salespeople's weekly meetings to gatherings among Christians resisting Roman rule. This drove home the importance of a mutually supportive sales

force and imbued the work with a sense of heroic mission.

4. **Connect emotionally.** Adjust your own emotional tone to match your audience's ability to receive your message. Learn how your colleagues have interpreted past events in the organization and sense how they will probably interpret your proposal. Test key individuals' possible reactions.

> *Example:* A Chrysler team leader raised the morale of employees disheartened by foreign competition when he persuaded senior management to bring a new car design in-house. He showed both groups slides of his hometown, devastated by foreign mining competition. Dramatic images of his boarded-up high school and the town's crumbling ironworks shone a sobering light on the aftereffects of outsourcing. His patriotic and emotional appeal resonated with his audiences.

Jay A. Conger is a professor of organizational behavior at the University of Southern California's Marshall School of Business in Los Angeles, where he directs the Leadership Institute. He is the author of *Winning 'Em Over: A New Model for Managing in the Age of Persuasion* (Simon & Schuster, 2001).

Three Ways *Not* to Persuade

by Jay A. Conger

In my work with managers as a researcher and as a consultant, I've had the unfortunate opportunity to see executives fail miserably at persuasion. Here are three of the most common mistakes people make:

1. **They attempt to make their case with an up-front, hard sell.** I call this the John Wayne approach. Managers strongly state their position at the outset, and then through a process of persistence, logic, and exuberance, they try to push the idea to a close. In reality, setting out a strong position at the start of a persuasion effort gives potential opponents something to grab onto—and fight against. It's far better

---

Excerpted from "The Necessary Art of Persuasion," by Jay A. Conger, *Harvard Business Review*, February 2000 (product #4258)

to present your position with the finesse
and reserve of a lion tamer, who engages his
"partner" by showing him the legs of a chair. In
other words, effective persuaders don't begin
the process by giving their colleagues a clear
target in which to set their jaws.

2. **They resist compromise.** Too many managers
   see compromise as surrender, but it is essential to constructive persuasion. Before people
   buy into a proposal, they want to see that the
   persuader is flexible enough to respond to their
   concerns. Compromises can often lead to better, more sustainable shared solutions.

   By not compromising, ineffective persuaders unconsciously send the message that they
   think persuasion is a one-way street. But persuasion is a process of give-and-take. Kathleen
   Reardon, a professor of organizational behavior at the University of Southern California,
   points out that a persuader rarely changes
   another person's behavior or viewpoint without
   altering his or her own in the process. To persuade meaningfully, we must not only listen to
   others but also incorporate their perspectives
   into our own.

3. **They assume persuasion is a one-shot effort.**
   Persuasion is a process, not an event. Rarely, if
   ever, is it possible to arrive at a shared solution
   on the first try. More often than not, persuasion involves listening to people, testing a posi-

tion, developing a new position that reflects input from the group, more testing, incorporating compromises, and then trying again. If this sounds like a slow and difficult process, that's because it is. But the results are worth the effort.

———————

Jay A. Conger is a professor of organizational behavior at the University of Southern California's Marshall School of Business in Los Angeles, where he directs the Leadership Institute. He is the author of *Winning 'Em Over: A New Model for Managing in the Age of Persuasion* (Simon & Schuster, 2001).

Harnessing the Science of Persuasion

A summary of the full-length HBR article by **Robert B. Cialdini,** *highlighting key ideas.*

THE IDEA IN BRIEF

Do you have it—the power to capture your audience, sway undecideds, convert opponents? In matrixed organizations, persuasion trumps formal power. It's essential to getting things done through others.

Persuasion works by appealing predictably to deeply rooted human needs. We can all learn to secure consensus, cut deals, win concessions—by artfully applying six scientific principles of winning friends and influencing people.

Reprint #R0109D

THE IDEA IN PRACTICE

Persuasion Principles

Principle	Example	Business Application
Liking: People like those like them, who like them.	At Tupperware parties, guests' fondness for their host influences purchase decisions twice as much as regard for the products.	**To influence people, win friends** through: • *Similarity*: Create *early* bonds with new peers, bosses, and direct reports by informally discovering common interests—you'll establish goodwill and trustworthiness. • *Praise*: Charm *and* disarm. Make positive remarks about others—you'll generate more willing compliance.
Reciprocity: People repay in kind.	When the Disabled American Veterans enclosed free personalized address labels in donation-request envelopes, response rate doubled.	**Give what you want to receive.** Lend a staff member to a colleague who needs help; you'll get *his* help later.
Social Proof: People follow the lead of similar others.	More New York City residents tried returning a lost wallet after learning that other New Yorkers had tried.	**Use peer power** to influence horizontally, not vertically; e.g., ask an esteemed "old timer" to support your new initiative if other veterans resist.
Consistency: People fulfill written, public, and voluntary commitments.	92% of residents of an apartment complex who signed a petition supporting a new recreation center later donated money to the cause.	**Make others' commitments active, public, and voluntary.** If you supervise an employee who should submit reports on time, get that understanding in writing (a memo); make the commitment public (note colleagues' agreement with the memo); and link the commitment to the employee's values (the impact of timely reports on team spirit).

Authority: People defer to experts who provide shortcuts to decisions requiring specialized information.	A single *New York Times* expert-opinion news story aired on TV generates a 4% shift in U.S. public opinion.	**Don't assume your expertise is self-evident.** Instead, establish your expertise *before* doing business with new colleagues or partners; e.g., in conversations before an important meeting, describe how you solved a problem similar to the one on the agenda.
Scarcity: People value what's scarce.	Wholesale beef buyers' orders jumped 600% when they alone received information on a possible beef shortage.	**Use exclusive information to persuade.** Influence and rivet key players' attention by saying, for example: "...Just got this information today. It won't be distributed until next week."

Robert B. Cialdini is the Regents' Professor of Psychology at Arizona State University and the author of *Influence: Science and Practice* (Allyn & Bacon, 2001). Further regularly updated information about the influence process can be found at http://www.influenceatwork.com/.

How to Get Your Colleagues' Attention

by Amy Gallo

Do you have to personally escort colleagues to your project meetings to make sure they show up? Does every "urgent" e-mail require phone or face-to-face follow-up to get a timely response? Do you have to hound your marketing partners to prioritize your products when they're launching new campaigns? These key tasks depend on your ability to **frame your message**—to make crystal clear what you need your colleagues to do, when, and, perhaps most important, why.

When you frame your message effectively, your audience will immediately understand the issue at hand and why it deserves their attention.

Here's how to frame your message to get the results you want, whether you're making a presentation, sending an e-mail, or talking in private with your boss:

- **Start with what you want.** Busy colleagues don't want to wait while you build to the punch line. Provide the most important information up front and ask for what you need.

  Example: "John, I need your advice about the product launch. I've gotten some new marketing data that may influence which message we lead with. I've come up with two alternatives, and I'd like your help deciding which to go with."

- **Set the scene.** Don't dive too deep into details, but provide enough context so your audience can follow along.

  Example: "To refresh your memory, the event we have planned is a question-and-answer panel on how to connect with today's modern moms. So far we've got five participants signed up to speak, including two CEOs of our top customers. Our goal is to reach as many marketers in the New York area as we can. We've sent out 2,500 invites and the initial response has been positive."

- **Explain the complication.** This is the specific reason for the meeting or your e-mail. What prompted you to deliver the message?

  Example: "As of today, the vendor is two weeks late with the prototypes. If there are further delays, we risk missing the deadline we set with the marketing team. We are somewhat stuck because the vendor knows we can't start over at this point with someone new. We need to figure out how to motivate the vendor and adjust our schedule so we can meet marketing's deadline."

- **Connect to the big picture.** Why should your audience care? Point out what is relevant to them and how it links to their broader goals.

   Example: "While eliminating the call checklist may seem like a small issue, it has important implications. It will encourage reps to engage with customers in a more informal way, which has been shown to increase customer satisfaction. This is a critical step toward meeting our unit's goal of 65% customer retention."

- **Make it memorable.** People hear news and information all day. Give them something to latch on to such as a metaphor, a key statistic, or a sound bite.

   Example: "Our customers feel this is an urgent issue and have told us so repeatedly. The longer we wait to respond, the more it will seem that the house is on fire and we're busy rearranging the furniture instead of calling 911."

- **Refocus your audience's attention.** It's easy for audiences to get distracted by secondary issues, so you must help them concentrate on the central objective. This is especially useful when you need to keep a large group on track or motivate people toward a common goal.

Example: "Susan, I see that you're concerned about getting the templates to design by our agreed-upon deadline. We need to make sure that happens. But let's agree on the right approach first—to be sure we're handing off a good product—and then we can work backwards to make sure we meet our deadlines."

- **End with a call to action.** Once you've set the context, reiterate what it is you need from your audience.

  Example: "Today I need to get your feedback on the presentation. I'd like to know specifically how we should tweak our high-level message to ensure it resonates with the leadership team."

  ———————

Amy Gallo is a contributing editor at *Harvard Business Review*. Follow her on Twitter at @amyegallo.

Collaborating Across Generations

by Tamara Erickson

If you work with people from every generation, as many of us do these days, how do you communicate with them? And how do you get them to support and participate in your initiatives? By understanding their priorities and positioning your ideas and requests accordingly. To help with that challenge, here's a snapshot of each generation, along with tips for working effectively across the ages.

Group	Defining characteristics	How to work with them
Boomers (born between 1946 and 1960)	• Hold a deeply competitive world view; see most scenarios as win-lose • Are hardworking and driven • Value individual achievement and recognition • Question authority and hierarchy, yet feel pressure to follow established rules and procedures • Are idealistic, but have by and large put "lofty" personal goals on the back burner for the past 30 years • Are often parents of Gen Ys and inclined to enjoy members of this generation • Enjoy mentoring others and the idea of leaving a legacy	OVERALL: • **Emphasize winning:** Explain how your idea either represents a "win" or will make the organization (or individual) more competitive. For instance, if you're offering a Boomer a new position in the company, comment on how you've chosen her over numerous other candidates. Or if you're proposing a new marketing investment, discuss how it will thwart a competitor's program. • **Seek their counsel:** Appeal to their desire to pass on their knowledge. You might ask a Boomer for advice on how to get her boss's attention, for example, or for help analyzing a problem that keeps cropping up.
		IF YOU'RE A GEN XER: • **Spell out your career goals:** Clearly convey your aspirations to any Boomers with influence on your career well before you're up for a promotion or new role. Don't assume they'll automatically know where you'd like to end up long term or what kind of development path you'd prefer. Their well-intentioned ideas may be quite different from your own. • **Overcommunicate:** Be transparent in your approach to projects or problem solving. You're more likely than your Boomer colleagues to consider multiple options. Explain how and when you'll make decisions so Boomers will recognize the time

Group	Defining characteristics	How to work with them
		you're spending as due diligence, not misconstrue it as indecision or procrastination. • **Partner with them:** Tap their experience and networks. For example, invite a Boomer to join your skunkworks team. When you're ready to pitch the best ideas to your executive board, she can help socialize the top contenders with her peers, which may help speed buy-in. She can also raise potential concerns early on—helping you dodge delays at the implementation phase.
		IF YOU'RE A GEN Y: • **Ask them for mentoring:** Pair your enthusiasm for learning with a Boomer's expertise and desire to give back. For example, share your most pressing project management problems with him and discuss potential solutions. In return, offer him tutorials on social media or time-saving technologies. • **Make sure your written communication is professional:** Boomers are more likely than others to base judgments on the way you present your ideas. Express your recommendations concisely, using correct grammar and spelling. Describe the financial benefits of your suggestions when possible.
Gen Xers (born between early 1960s and late 1970s)	• Are self-reliant • Don't trust any institution (corporations,	OVERALL: • **Weigh your options:** Most Xers want to know that you've considered *(continued)*

Group	Defining characteristics	How to work with them
	marriage, and so on) to take care of them forever • Like to keep their options open • Are irreverent • Think outside the box and are comfortable changing the rules as necessary • Accept the validity of diverse points of view • Have close relationships within a small group of friends (their "tribe") • Place high priority on being good parents	contingencies. Earn their respect and buy-in by including a discussion of "what if" when you present ideas to them. For instance, identify the two or three events or trends that would be most likely to disrupt your proposed course of action—and the response you would recommend taking if each one were to occur. • **Let them choose:** Whenever possible, present a menu of solutions and engage the Xer (whether she is your boss, colleague, or subordinate) in the process of choosing the best one. You might, for example, ask her what weight she would give to various decision criteria.
		IF YOU'RE A BOOMER: • **Employ their innovative thinking:** Ask an Xer to help solve a problem or reality-check your solution to make sure you're viewing the challenge from every possible angle. For example, invite him to test the validity of your strategy statement by posing a broad range of scenarios you might not have considered on your own. • **Harness their ability to integrate multiple points of view:** Invite an Xer to lead a complex group discussion—for instance, an after-action review. She's likely to ensure that everyone is heard so you'll have a fuller picture of what worked well and what needs improvement.

Group	Defining characteristics	How to work with them
		IF YOU'RE A GEN Y: • **Explore common ground:** Make the most of your shared passion for discovering new ways of working. For example, ask an Xer to help you analyze and improve your cross-functional team's processes. Or work together to find opportunities to leverage new technology in the organization. • **Respect the dues they've paid:** Most Xers have worked their way up a long career track and may feel threatened by the perception that you want to "leapfrog" past them. When you express your desire for more challenging work, be clear that you're not looking to take their seat.
Gen Ys (born between 1980 and the mid-1990s)	• Expect to live life fully each day • Are optimistic and confident • Prefer to work on their schedule, not yours • Are hungry to learn; expect regular coaching • Get things done using in-the-moment coordination rather than long-range planning • Work collaboratively • Have limited awareness of corporate hierarchy and protocol • Are comfortable expressing opinions freely and bluntly • Enjoy and respect their parents and tend to retain close relationships with them	OVERALL: • **Ramp up the challenge:** Give stretch assignments to maintain their interest. For example, ask a Gen Y to prepare a draft proposal for a client. You'll free up more of your time for other priorities, and he'll feel that he's making career progress. Or specify an outcome you need to achieve, but leave the approach to his discretion. Encourage him to find ways to do it better. Tell him, for instance, that the sales team needs to understand and get excited about a new product's features by the planned launch date, but invite him to propose the communication and training plan. *(continued)*

Group	Defining characteristics	How to work with them
		• **Put their work into context:** Explain how what they do affects the larger organization. For example, invite a Gen Y to your next marketing meeting so she can see how the daily sales dashboard she's setting up will help your group accurately track the impact of different campaigns. • **Provide frequent feedback:** Take every opportunity to teach them. After a brainstorming session, for instance, pull your Gen Y direct report aside to note how useful it was for him to help facilitate. Give him a few specific suggestions on how he could do it even more effectively next time.
		IF YOU'RE A BOOMER: • **Clarify how you'll communicate with each other:** Agree on "rules" everyone feels comfortable with. For example: How frequently will you exchange e-mails or text messages? Will you share questions and thoughts as they come to mind or save them for a weekly status meeting? Work together to accommodate your different preferences. • **Tap their technological prowess:** Gen Ys are great sources of tech support, often without realizing it. Task a Gen Y with test-driving new software, for example, or looking for shortcuts in the sales-reporting process.

Group	Defining characteristics	How to work with them
		IF YOU'RE A GEN XER: • **Invite Boomers to teach them:** If you have a number of Gen Ys reporting to you, facilitate mentoring relationships between them and Boomers, who enjoy teaching and tend to click with Ys (more so than many Xers). Don't assume that all demands for coaching must be met by the Ys' managers—spread the responsibilities among other experienced colleagues. • **Clear up ambiguities:** Ys often ask their managers, typically Xers, for things in terms that can be easily misunderstood. For example, "I'd like a bigger job" may simply mean that a Y wants something more challenging, not necessarily that she's angling for a promotion. If a Y says, "I'd like to do multiple jobs this year," she's probably talking about a variety of tasks, not formal job assignments. "Feedback" often means teaching, not critique or blanket praise. If you're not 100% sure what a Y means, ask her to clarify.

Tamara Erickson wrote a trilogy of books on the generations: *Retire Retirement, Plugged In,* and *What's Next, Gen X?*. She was named one of the 50 leading management thinkers in 2009 and 2011 by Thinkers50.

When the Direct Approach Backfires, Try Indirect Influence

by Martha Craumer

How do you get people who don't work for you to *work for you*?

When direct management techniques don't work—especially with those over whom you have no authority—you may have better luck with these, more subtle, approaches.

1. **Talk less, listen more.** When you try to persuade people, you can spend too much time explaining your position, and not enough time asking questions, listening, and understanding other points of view.

Adapted from reprint #U0608D

Your colleagues are less likely to resist when they feel you've taken the time to acknowledge their concerns. In *The 7 Habits of Highly Effective People*, Stephen Covey says that the greatest need of human beings—after physical survival—is to be understood, affirmed, and appreciated. He explains that "empathic listening gets inside another person's frame of reference. You look out through it, you see the world the way they [do], you understand their paradigm, you understand how they feel." It's human nature to want to work with, not against, someone who "gets" us. Ask about your colleagues' challenges or people they're struggling with. This information will help you identify common goals and solutions. And you'll be building stronger working relationships.

2. **Make 'em like you.** It's hard to say no to someone you like. So how can you increase your likability? Play up similarities. We tend to like people who share our background, interests, style of dress, etc.

    We also like people who like us. We're suckers for compliments. If your colleague does a good job leading a meeting, tell him what you liked about the way he ran it. Be specific. Ask another colleague about her weekend and listen—perhaps you'll discover a shared passion for hiking or reading. Then when you need their help, your colleagues will be more likely to offer their expertise.

3. **Make 'em laugh.** Ever wonder why so many speakers open their presentations with a joke? Humor is disarming. It makes people root for us. It's hard to feel bad when you're laughing—and hard to dislike a person who makes you laugh.

   Humor makes you appear calm, approachable, and in control. It helps your audience feel more relaxed and receptive to change, new ideas, and your influence. Use humor to help soften a harsh message and make it easier to speak freely about the challenge at hand.

   But use humor with care. Inside jokes and cultural allusions can be off-putting. And, of course, humor should never be at the expense of the person you're trying to influence—nor should it make light of her issues or concerns.

4. **Do a favor—even a small one.** Doing something for someone gives you enormous power and influence over them. In his book *Influence: The Psychology of Persuasion*, Robert Cialdini discusses the unwritten rule of reciprocity and how it obligates us to repay what another person has given us.

   Cialdini cites a research study involving two groups of subjects and a "plant"—a man named Joe—who was posing as a fellow subject. Each member of the first group received a small "favor" from Joe—a Coke that he picked up for them while out of the room. The second group received no favor. Then, Joe told each group he was selling raffle tickets. The subjects who received a Coke from Joe bought twice as many tickets as the subjects who received nothing. The reciprocity rule overwhelmed all other factors—including whether they even liked Joe. The ticket buyers felt an irresistible need to repay him.

The more you raise your hand to help others, the more likely they'll do the same for you. Volunteer to take notes at a colleague's brainstorming session. Help set out lunch for a big client meeting. Offer to listen to your teammate's dry run of a big presentation.

5. **Feed 'em.** Pick up an extra coffee for the programmer who's been developing a data feed for your new website. Bring fresh fruit or candy bars to your project launch meeting. Pick one day every two weeks to take a colleague to lunch. Don't ask your buddy—invite people whom you don't often get to see outside of all-staff meetings, to help deepen your relationships and extend your network. It's simple, but true: we like to be fed.

Martha Craumer is a freelance writer based in Cambridge, Massachusetts.

Index

Notes

Notes

Notes

Notes